This book

the Mosier children

It was given to you by

Pat Brawner

Date

August 19, 2014

"With loving thoughts ..."

DAILY DEVOTIONAL FOR KIDS!

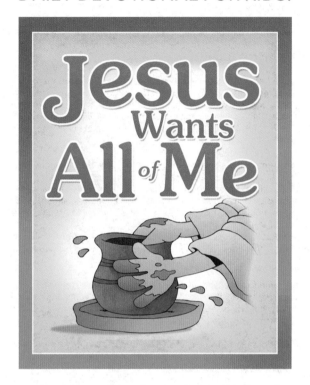

Jesus Wants All of Me

Based on the Golden Book of Oswald Chambers
MY UTMOST FOR HIS HIGHEST

Adapted and Illustrated by
PHIL A. SMOUSE

Authorized by the Oswald Chambers Association, Ltd.

BARBOUR
PUBLISHING

ISBN 978-1-61626-678-3

Published by Barbour Publishing, Inc., P.O. Box 719, Uhrichsville, Ohio 44683
www.barbourbooks.com

Our mission is to publish and distribute inspirational products offering exceptional value and biblical encouragement to the masses.

Member of the
Evangelical Christian
Publishers Association

Printed in the United States of America.
Versa Press, Inc., East Peoria, IL 61611; July 2013; D10004017

For Maurice
and for "purity of motive."

To the Parent

"I am determined to be absolutely
and entirely for Him and for Him alone."

Oswald Chambers

Oswald Chambers understood the secret of the Christian life—that he must give himself completely to God. And because he did, God has used Oswald Chambers' book, **My Utmost for His Highest**, to draw millions of readers into a deeper relationship with Himself.

God wants the very same from each of us. He wants us to be His—100 percent. And the most important thing is not what we say or do, or even who we reach. The most important thing is the relationship we cultivate with Him.

That deep spiritual connection isn't only for adults. In fact, Jesus Himself talked about having a childlike faith. **Jesus Wants All of Me,** based on Chambers' classic devotional, can be your guide as a parent to help your children develop a deeper relationship with God. These daily thoughts will teach your children truths from God's Word that will stay with them the rest of their lives.

What could be more important than that? Use this devotional to help your children meet—and give their hearts to—Jesus.

Phil A. Smouse

Jesus Wants All of Me

January 1

I am God's. My heart is His heart. My mind is His mind. My eyes will look for Him. My ears will listen for His voice. My hands will do His will. I am God's!

I trust that my life will bring honor to Christ.

Philippians 1:20 NLT

Where Are We Going?

January 2

God knows what will happen tomorrow. He knows where I will be. He knows what I will do. I don't have to worry. I am in good hands. I am in *God's* hands!

He went out, not knowing where he was going.

Hebrews 11:8

I Can See Clearly Now

January 3

I can talk to God. And God can talk to me! God speaks to me from His Word. His Word is the Bible. God's Spirit inside of me will help me understand what the Bible says. When God speaks, I will listen.

Clouds and darkness surround Him.

Psalm 97:2

Wait for Me!

January 4

God answers my prayers. At times He says, "Yes." Other times He says, "No." And every now and then God will say, "Wait." I don't like to wait. But if God says, "Wait," I will wait. I won't run ahead of Him. I will follow.

> "Lord, why can't
> I follow you now?"
>
> John 13:37 NIV

Follow the Leader

January 5

I will follow Jesus. I don't have to make promises to Him. I know I won't always understand. I don't need to be perfect. I only need to follow Him. Jesus loves me.

"You will follow me later."

John 13:36 NLT

Give It Back!

January 6

What is the very best thing God has ever given to me? God wants me to give it back! He wants me to share that gift with someone else. That's why He gave it to me. I won't keep God's gift to myself. I will give it back!

There he built an altar to the LORD.

Genesis 12:8

Do I Know Him?

January 7

When I like someone, I want to spend time with that person. We do things together. That's what makes us friends. I want to spend time with God. I want to be best friends with Him.

"Have I been with you so long, and yet you have not known Me?"

John 14:9

I Give Up

January 8

God wants all of me. He wants me to give Him everything. Whatever I do, He wants me to be thinking about Him. God loves me!

And Abraham built an altar. . .
and he bound Isaac his son.

Genesis 22:9

So Big!

January 9

God made the morning and the evening. He made the mighty mountains. He made the oceans and everything in them. But God is brighter than the morning. He is higher than the mountains. His love for me is deeper than any ocean. God made me. And He will make me be like His Son. He will make me be like Jesus.

May your whole spirit and soul and body be kept blameless until our Lord Jesus Christ comes again.

1 Thessalonians 5:23 NLT

For Me?

January 10

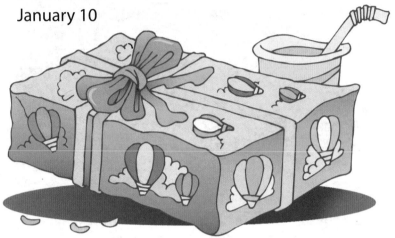

Jesus will give me a beautiful gift. He will take all my sins away. But how do I get His gift? Do I promise to be good? What do I have to do? I don't have to do anything! I just have to open my heart to Jesus.

"Open their eyes. . .
that they may receive."

Acts 26:18

Grumpy, Grumpy

January 11

Sometimes, when I obey the Bible, other people will feel upset. But God wants me to obey Him no matter what other people say or do. I don't like it when others are upset. But God will care for them. And I will let Him.

> . . .and on [Simon]
> they laid the cross.
>
> Luke 23:26

He Knows My Name

January 12

Why do I feel this way? Why can't I understand myself? I just don't know. But Jesus knows. He knows even when I don't. Maybe something is wrong. Maybe I need to change. I will let Jesus change my heart.

When they were alone,
He explained all things to His disciples.

Mark 4:34

Quiet, Please!

January 13

Sometimes I don't like to be alone. I feel lonely. But when I'm alone, everything is quiet. I can talk to God. If I listen, maybe I'll hear Him answer me.

When He was alone. . .
the twelve asked Him.

Mark 4:10

Called by God

January 14

People need to know about God's love. And God wants them to know. Someone should probably tell them! But who should it be? Whom has God picked? He has picked someone very special. He has picked me. He wants me to tell people that God loves them.

Then I said,
"Here am I! Send me."

Isaiah 6:8

Out with the Old

January 15

I am born again. God took the dirty, stinky things in me and buried them. They are gone! I won't dig them up. I don't want them back. God's love makes me new and clean.

We also should walk
in newness of life.

Romans 6:4

It's for You

January 16

God is calling me. He has a job for me to do!
What great thing should I do for Him? I know!
I will get down on my knees. I will listen for His
voice. I will find out what He wants. Then I
will get up and do it.

I heard the voice of the Lord,
saying: "Whom shall I send?"

Isaiah 6:8

Okay, I'm Coming!

January 17

God is calling me. He has a wonderful plan for my life. And I will do amazing things. But God wants me to *be* something much more than He wants me to *do* something. He wants me to be like His Son.

But when it pleased God. . .
to reveal His Son in me.

Galatians 1:15–16

That's Good!

January 18

I can do many good things for other people. I can help. I can listen. I can be a friend. I love to do good things. But I love God more than anything else.

Thomas answered and said to Him,
"My Lord and my God!"

John 20:28

Darkness

January 19

Sometimes I just don't understand. I feel like I'm all alone in the dark. Where is God? I can't find Him. I can't reach Him. I am so small, and He is so far away. But if I wait, God will show me that He is here with me. Maybe not right away, but He will show me. And when He does, I will see again. I will see His face. God is real.

Great darkness fell upon him.

Genesis 15:12

Ready for Everything

January 20

I am born again. Jesus made everything new.
I can do fun things. I can do difficult things.
And I can enjoy them both. God's love is alive in
my heart. When I'm close to God, I never feel bored.

"I tell you the truth, unless you
are born again, you cannot see
the Kingdom of God."

John 3:3 NLT

Now I Remember

January 21

Sometimes I forget that Jesus loves me.
But He shows me His love in a thousand ways.
Then I am so glad that He loves me. And, oh,
how I love Him.

"I remember you,
the kindness of your youth."

Jeremiah 2:2

Looking Up

January 22

Lord, You've given me so much—so much that I can't even see You anymore! Maybe I should stop looking at all the good things You've given me. Maybe I should set all this stuff aside and just start looking for You.

"Look to Me, and be saved."

Isaiah 45:22

Mirror, Mirror

January 23

When people look at me, what do they see? Do they see Jesus? I will take time to be with Him. When I spend more time with Jesus, I'll learn to act more like Him. I want to be like Jesus.

The Lord. . .makes us more and more like him as we are changed into his glorious image.

2 Corinthians 3:18 NLT

Take It Personally

January 24

I know about Jesus. I know that He died on the cross. I know that He rose again. I know that He washed my sins away. But I don't want to just know about Jesus. I want to be friends with Him. I want to *know* Him.

"I have appeared to you for this purpose."

Acts 26:16

Surprise!

January 25

God will answer my prayers. But not always the way I expect Him to! He may surprise me. He may not! Who knows what God will do? But God will answer my prayers. I know He will!

But when it pleased God. . .

Galatians 1:15

It's That Simple

January 26

God has my heart. He will take care of me. I will always have everything I need. It's just that simple. Thank You, Lord.

"He will certainly care for you."

Matthew 6:30 NLT

I Never Thought about It

January 27

What will I eat? What will I drink? What will I wear? And where will it all come from? I don't know. I never really thought about it. Anyway, Jesus told me not to worry about all that. He said He would take care of it.

"Do not worry about your life."

Matthew 6:25

My Way

January 28

I did it my way. I thought of everything by myself. I did all the work. I didn't ask anyone for help. And I was wrong! O Lord, I'm so sorry. I should have done it Your way.

"Saul, Saul, why are you persecuting Me?"

Acts 26:14

His Way
January 29

O Lord, I've made such a mess of things.
Everyone is angry. Everything is ruined.
My way doesn't work. I don't want my way
anymore. Please show me Your way.

"Who are
You, Lord?"

Acts 26:15

Who Said That?

January 30

I will pray. God will show me what to do. I know His voice. I hear Him in my heart. I see Him all around me. He will speak to me. And when He does, I will listen.

And Samuel was afraid to tell Eli the vision.

1 Samuel 3:15

Too Good to Be True

January 31

Oh, I can be good! I can look good. I can sound good. I can do good things. And that's good! But God doesn't care how good I act on the outside. He wants me to know Jesus on the inside.

. . .set apart
for the gospel of God.

Romans 1:1 NIV

Your Love

February 1

People hurt me sometimes. Things go wrong. But that's all right. Jesus will heal the people who hurt me. He will fix the messed up things. O Lord, here is my heart. Please let me tell someone about Your love.

For Christ did not send me to baptize, but to preach the gospel.

1 Corinthians 1:17

Who Cares?

February 2

Who cares about those people? Who cares if he knows Jesus? Who cares if she hears the Word of God? Who cares if someone tells him about God's love? Who cares if she finds God? Jesus cares. And so do I!

Woe is me
if I do not preach the gospel!

1 Corinthians 9:16

Bad People

February 3

I can't love them! They've done too many bad things! But Jesus loves even people who do bad things. They are His children. I've done bad things, too, but Jesus made me good. I will tell them that Jesus loves them.

> We have been made
> as the filth of the world.
>
> 1 Corinthians 4:13

Training Wheels

February 4

God does so much for me. He gives me so many good things. But God's blessings are like my training wheels. One day I won't need to lean on them anymore. Then I will really fly. All I need is Him!

For the love of Christ compels us.

2 Corinthians 5:14

Here Am I

February 5

No one may ever know about the good things I do. No one may ever hear about me. That's okay. I don't want to be famous. I don't need to be important. Jesus loves me. I will follow Him.

I am being poured out
as a drink offering.

Philippians 2:17

Here Is My Heart

February 6

Jesus, here is my heart. Please take away anything that makes You sad. I know it will hurt. But I will try not to cry. You will help me. You are everything that I ever dreamed You would be.

For I am
already being poured out.

2 Timothy 4:6

Are We There Yet?

February 7

I am so upset! I prayed and prayed. Why is God taking so long to answer? Didn't He hear me? Doesn't He care? Maybe I shouldn't be so worried about His answer. Maybe I should just get closer to Him.

"But it has already been three days."

Luke 24:21 CEV

Just Like You

February 8

Jesus, I want to be just like You. I want to see what You see. I want to feel what You feel. Come into my heart. Make my heart Your home. Make me just like You.

I pray that God, who gives peace, will make you completely holy.

1 Thessalonians 5:23 CEV

Tired of Being Good

February 9

Sometimes I get tired of being good. I feel worn out. But that's all right. God understands how I feel. He will help me to be good, even when I'm tired.

The everlasting God. . .
neither faints nor is weary.

Isaiah 40:28

There You Are

February 10

Lord, sometimes I can't imagine what You are like. But I want to be with You. Gentle breeze. Shining stars. Falling leaves. There You are, Lord. Everywhere I look, something reminds me of You.

Lift up your eyes on high, and see who has created these things.

Isaiah 40:26

Peace Like a River

February 11

God is bigger than me. He hung the stars in the sky. The sun shines with the light of His love. Every silver snowflake was made by the gentle touch of His hand. He will never leave me. I will trust in Him.

You will keep him in perfect peace, whose mind is stayed on You.

Isaiah 26:3

Do I Listen?

February 12

God speaks. But do I listen? He told me to love even people who are mean to me. I will go to church. I will be very quiet. I will even listen to the pastor. But love people who are mean to me? I can't do that! Yes, God speaks. But do I listen?

"You speak with us, and we will hear."

Exodus 20:19

Busy, Busy!
February 13

I am so very busy sometimes! I must do this!
I must do that! What's that, Lord? What did You
say? Speak up! I can't hear You! Oops! I have to
go now. Give me a call sometime. I'd really love
to talk to You. Bye!

"Speak, for Your servant hears."

1 Samuel 3:10

Stop, Look, Listen

February 14

Lord, where are You? I can't see You. I can't hear You. I don't know what to do. Please don't leave me here, God. I will be still. I will listen. I will wait. You will come.

"Whatever I tell you in the dark, speak in the light."

Matthew 10:27

My Brother's Keeper

February 15

I am not perfect. Sometimes I get angry. Sometimes I make mistakes. Sometimes I even hurt my friends. I don't want to hurt my friends. I will do something special for them. I will show them God loves them.

None of us
lives to himself.

Romans 14:7

I Must Get Up!

February 16

I give up! I am frustrated. My dreams will never come true. But God says, "Try again." He says, "Get up." He will help me. He will make them real. But first I must get up.

"Arise from the dead."

Ephesians 5:14

Get Going

February 17

I will get up. I will get going. There is no reason to be sad. Jesus is with me. He will work it out. Everything will be okay. I think I'll make my bed and go get a cookie.

"Arise and eat."

1 Kings 19:5

Don't Look Back

February 18

Oh no! What have I done? It's just no use. I've ruined everything! But Jesus will forgive me. He will take my awful mistakes and send them far away! I will give Jesus my broken heart. I will not look back. I will get up. I will take His hand. I will begin again.

"Rise,
let us be going."

Matthew 26:46

Shine

February 19

What do I have to do today? Is it the very same thing I did yesterday? Will I do it all over again tomorrow? Whatever it may be—here are my hands, Lord. You take them. Help me make something beautiful.

Arise, shine.

Isaiah 60:1

Dreaming

February 20

God gave me a wonderful dream! Oh, the places I'll go! Oh, the people I'll meet! I'd like to dream like this forever. But now it's time to wake up. It's time to do it!

"Arise,
let us go from here."

John 14:31

Now I've Done It!

February 21

Oh dear. Now I've done it. Just look at me!
And look at this mess! I know I should try to
be more careful. But I just got so excited. I love
You so much. I had to show You! I know You
understand. Even when I get too excited,
You can use me.

"She has done
a good work for Me."

Mark 14:6

Let Go!

February 22

I'm strong. I'm tough. I'm hanging in there. I've tied a knot at the end of my rope, and I'm hanging on! But did God tell me to hang on? Or am I just afraid to let go?

Be still, and know that I am God.

Psalm 46:10

When People Hurt Me

February 23

When I'm selfish I break God's heart. But Jesus forgives me. He spread out His arms and died for me. People may hurt me. They may even make me cry. But that's okay. I hurt Jesus. But He died to take my sins away. He forgave me. I will forgive the people who hurt me.

The Son of Man did not come to be served, but to serve.

Matthew 20:28

Help Yourself!

February 24

Here is my life, Jesus. I will go where You want me to go. I will do what You want me to do. You can have whatever You want, Lord. Just help Yourself—to me!

I will very gladly spend and be spent for your souls.

2 Corinthians 12:15

They Love Me Not

February 25

I want to tell them about Jesus. But what if they get mad at me? What if they laugh? What if they won't love me anymore? Oh, who cares if they love me or not? I love them. And I want them to know Jesus.

It seems that the more I love you, the less you love me.

2 Corinthians 12:15 NLT

You Can't Be Serious!

February 26

You want me to do what, God? I can't do that! It will never work! And how will I ever get it done? O God, when will I ever learn to trust You? And how long will it be before I realize that You can do what I cannot?

"Sir, You have nothing
to draw with."

John 4:11

Troubled Water

February 27

Why do I feel this way? Why does it hurt so much? Why won't anyone help? Maybe I should try to be strong. Maybe I should just try to do this by myself. No! I feel too empty inside. Only Jesus can help. He is God Almighty. And I will look to Him.

"Where then do You get that living water?"

John 4:11

What's the Big Idea?

February 28

I will do great things for God! I will dream up a big idea. I will ask God to bless it! It will be big. It will be new! And it will be wrong! Please forgive me, Jesus. I put my big idea in Your place inside my heart. Something will always go wrong with my big ideas. But I believe in You.

Jesus answered them, "Do you now believe?"

John 16:31

Mission Impossible

February 29

I can't ask God to do that. That would be impossible! You're right. No one could do that. No one but God. Go ahead. Ask Him to do it! God will do the impossible.

"Lord, that I may receive my sight."

Luke 18:41

Do I Love Him?

March 1

I can do good. I can be good. Everyone may think well of me. And I can say that I love Him. But do I *really* love Him?

"Do you love Me?"

John 21:17

Yes, I Love Him

March 2

It hurt when Jesus said, "Do you love Me?"
Why would He say that? He knows I love Him.
He knows I do! But that is why He asked. He
knows. And now I know, too!

He said to him the third time,
"Do you love Me?"

John 21:17

Feed My Sheep

March 3

Yes, Lord. I do love You! Now I will feed Your sheep. You have some funny sheep. But I will love them all. I will love every lumpy, dirty, lost, last one of them.

"Feed My sheep."

John 21:17

Father Knows Best

March 4

Where can God use me? What does He want me to do? I am good at many things. Things that would be very useful. But God does not care if I'm useful. He wants me to love Him. He wants me to be His.

"Nor do I count my life dear to myself."

Acts 20:24

Well Done!

March 5

God has a job for me. So I will do it! I may not be the very best. I may not always get it right. It may not go the way I planned. But God isn't worried about that. He just wants me to do it. He wants me to show Him I love Him.

". . .so that I may finish
my race with joy."

Acts 20:24

Same Old Thing

March 6

Nothing new today. No big plans. Nothing much going on. No one watching to see what I will do. Just You and me. Just like yesterday. Thank You, Jesus. Thank You for making the same old thing special.

. . .in much patience. . .

2 Corinthians 6:4

Surf's Up

March 7

Trouble will come. But I will not be afraid. The wind will blow. The waves will crash. I will not run away. I will grab my surfboard. I will run for the water. I will stand up and ride. Whee! Nothing can separate me from the love of God.

We are more than conquerors through Him who loved us.

Romans 8:37

What God Wants

March 8

What does God want? Does He want my kindness? My honesty? My good deeds? No. He wants my sin. God wants to take my sin away and put Jesus in its place.

"I have been crucified with Christ."

Galatians 2:20

He Went That Way

March 9

I will walk with Jesus. I will go when He says, "Go." I will stop when He says, "Stop." I don't need to figure it all out. Jesus loves me. I can trust Him. He will lead me home.

"Do you also want to go away?"

John 6:67

Be a Message

March 10

God gave me a message. He gave me His Word. And the Word of God can change lives. But first it must change me. Yes, God gave me a message. And if I let Him, He will make me a message, too. My life will tell everyone that God loves them.

Preach the word!

2 Timothy 4:2

What God Sees

March 11

I know God has a plan for me. And He will make it happen. It may take a long time. But I can wait. I will let Jesus plant me, just like a seed. Sometimes a seed takes a long time to grow. But God knows the right time. One day I will blossom and bring forth fruit.

"I was not disobedient to the heavenly vision. . ."

Acts 26:19

What's in It for Me?

March 12

I love to give. I would give Jesus anything. Even myself. For He always gives so much in return. But I will not treat Jesus like a bubble-gum machine. I love Him for who He is. Not for what I get out of Him.

"See, we have left all
and followed You."

Mark 10:28

Clean!

March 13

I can be good. I can obey. I can mind my manners. But I need to do something even more important. I can forget about me and get caught up in the wonder of Jesus! I can give myself to Him. Just like He gave me Himself.

"God so loved the world that He gave. . ."

John 3:16

Who Has My Heart?

March 14

Who has my heart? What have I given it to?
Have I given it to anger? To being important?
To having lots of things? Jesus made my heart.
But have I given it back to Him?

You become the slave
of whatever you choose to obey.

Romans 6:16 NLT

Where Are We Going?

March 15

Where are we going? What is Jesus doing? Why doesn't He stop? Why won't He wait? Why has He gone so far ahead? I thought I knew Him. I thought He loved me. How can I follow Him now? O Lord, forgive me. It is so dark. And I am so afraid. I will be still. I will trust You. You are God.

And as they followed
they were afraid.

Mark 10:32

Into the Light

March 16

What am I hiding? What lives deep down in the secret darkness of my heart? Is it anger? Unforgiveness? Do I want to hurt my friend? I will drag those things out into God's light. I will let Him change my heart.

For we must all appear
before the judgment seat of Christ.

2 Corinthians 5:10

First Things First

March 17

I want to do good. I want to help. I want to share God's love. I want to tell others about Jesus. But I will not give my heart to any of these things. My heart belongs to Jesus.

Therefore we make it our aim. . .
to be well pleasing to Him.

2 Corinthians 5:9

Have It Your Way

March 18

How do I look? What do you see? Do you see Jesus—or do you see me? I will let Jesus wash me. Jesus knows where I need to be washed inside. I know, too. And I want to be clean.

> . . .perfecting holiness
> out of reverence for God.
>
> 2 Corinthians 7:1 NIV

Lead Me On
March 19

Where are we going? I don't really know! But God knows. And I know Him. So I will keep on walking. God is real. God is here. Jesus loves me. Everything will be all right.

He went out, not knowing where he was going.

Hebrews 11:8

Decisions, Decisions!

March 20

What does God want? What is God's will?
God's will is me! And He has set me free.
I am not afraid to decide. Jesus loves me.
If I am wrong, He will show me. And I will stop.

"Shall I hide from Abraham
what I am doing?"

Genesis 18:17

I'm with Him

March 21

Jesus died on the cross to take away my sins. He did it for me. And now He wants to live in me, too. Please come into my heart, Lord Jesus. Oh, how I love You.

"I have been crucified with Christ."

Galatians 2:20

A Burning Heart

March 22

God's love is like a fire burning in my heart.
It lights up every dreary place. It melts the
coldest frozen heart. Its gentle warmth and
beautiful fragrance are the light and life of
every plain old, bald, and boring day.

"Didn't our hearts burn within us
as he talked with us?"

Luke 24:32 NLT

I Was Wrong

March 23

I was wrong. I know what I did. I know it was a mistake. I did it anyway. But I won't make excuses. There's nothing to explain. Please forgive me. I was wrong.

Since there is jealousy
and quarreling among you,
are you not. . .acting like mere humans?

1 Corinthians 3:3 NIV

Let It Happen

March 24

I told her about Jesus. And she got mad! I know
God is changing her heart. And that hurts. I'd
like to make it better. But I won't. I will get out
of God's way. I will let God plow her up so He
can plant new seed in her. Soon Jesus will
grow tall and strong in her broken heart.

"He must increase,
but I must decrease."

John 3:30

Don't Look at Me

March 25

I want to be good. I want to be kind. But not so you will look at me. Not even to show you what God can do. Was I standing in front of Jesus? I'm sorry. I will sit down. Now maybe you can see Him.

The friend of
the bridegroom. . .

John 3:29

Pure in Heart

March 26

I can't do that anymore. It's not really bad. It's not really wrong. But it just doesn't feel right. I guess it's okay for other people. But when I do it, I feel like I've broken God's heart. I'm just not going to do that anymore.

"Blessed are the pure in heart,
for they shall see God."

Matthew 5:8

Good Enough Yet?

March 27

Am I good enough yet? Am I doing all right? I could be more polite. I could read more and pray more and give more and do more. But most of all, I could look to Jesus more. Then I could get to know Him better.

"Come up here! I will show you what must happen next."

Revelation 4:1 CEV

Faith

March 28

I know what God wants. But how will I do it? I can study and plan. I can think through the good and bad. But that is not faith. I don't understand. But God does. I can trust Him. He loves me. I will do what He says. I feel happy inside when I follow Him.

> The disciples said to Him,
> ". . .are You going there again?"
>
> John 11:8

Knock, Knock

March 29

Surprise! Where will I find Jesus today? Who knows? He could be anywhere! In anything or anyone. His love is bigger than my church. Bigger than my ideas. Bigger than any endless winter sky. He is alive inside of my heart. I will look for Him everywhere.

"Therefore you also
be ready."

Luke 12:40

I Will Pray

March 30

I will pray for her. I will not get angry. I will not
talk behind her back. I think something must
be wrong. Something is breaking her heart.
I will ask God to help her. I know God has
a plan for her life. And He wants me to help—
He wants me to pray for her.

He was surprised
that there was no one to help.

Isaiah 59:16 NCV

Me First

March 31

God will fix him! He's creepy and mean and he never says anything nice, and he just makes me so mad! Yes, God will fix him! But maybe God should fix me first. Then I can pray for this person.

If anyone
sees his brother sinning. . .

1 John 5:16

Have a Heart

April 1

God's Word can change the hardest heart. But I will not use it like a spear to stab my enemy. I will speak God's truth with love. And then I will remember to pray.

All of our thoughts are known to God. . .as the Spirit prays for God's people.

Romans 8:27 CEV

Now I See

April 2

Once I couldn't see Jesus. I wanted to have lots of things. I wanted people to like me. I wanted everyone to do what I said. But something happened. I put all that down. And now I can see. Now I can see Jesus.

"The Lord Jesus
. . .has sent me that you may
receive your sight."

Acts 9:17

If Only
April 3

Why did I do that? What was I thinking? How can God love me when I make the same awful mistakes over and over again? I don't want to think about it! But I must. And then I must let Him change my heart.

"If you had known. . .the things that make for your peace!"

Luke 19:42

Trust or Bust

April 4

Where did God go? Why isn't He blessing my plans? How can I trust Him if He won't bless me? How can I trust Him if He won't make me happy? How can I say that I love Him when all I care about are His blessings?

"Indeed the hour is coming. . .
that you will be scattered."

John 16:32

Gethsemane

April 5

Jesus was alone in the garden. But why was He crying? It was my sin. He knew He was about to die. He knew He would be nailed to the cross. But He did nothing wrong! It was all my fault. He would die because of my sins. And His death would take my sins away! How could He love me that much? I don't know. But He did. Jesus is God's Son. But He lived as a man. He died as a man. And because He did, I will see the face of God.

Jesus came with them
to. . .Gethsemane.

Matthew 26:36

The Cross

April 6

Jesus was born to die on the cross. It was not an accident. It did not happen to Him. Jesus went there on purpose. He went there for me.

. . .who Himself bore our sins
in His own body on the tree.

1 Peter 2:24

Show and Tell

April 7

The Bible can be hard to understand. And God's heart can be hard to find. But God is not hiding from me. He is calling me closer. When I dare to look for Him, the flower of His Word will begin to bloom inside of my heart.

He commanded them
that they should tell no one
the things they had seen.

Mark 9:9

To Rise Again

April 8

Jesus died on the cross. But He rose again! God gave Him new life. Now Jesus wants to give His new life to me. He wants to nail my sin to the cross. He wants to leave it there to die. He wants to put His life in its place. He wants to make me His child.

"Did not the Messiah
have to suffer these things. . . ?"

Luke 24:26

Have I Seen Him?

April 9

God is good. I have everything I need. I see His blessings each and every day. But have I ever looked beyond His blessings? Beyond what He gives? Have I ever seen Him? I want to see Jesus.

He appeared in another form to two of them.

Mark 16:12

What to Do with Sin

April 10

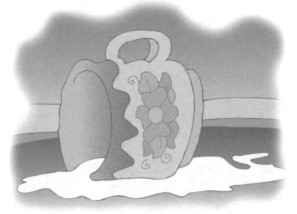

Sin is anything that breaks God's heart. And I have sinned. But what should I do about it? Should I try to quit? Should I find something better to do? No! My sin must be killed! I must let God nail it to the cross.

We know that our old sinful selves were crucified with Christ so that sin might lose its power in our lives.

Romans 6:6 NLT

Come On In!

April 11

Here is my heart, Jesus. Please make my heart Your home. Fill every closet and cupboard. Invade every dark and empty room with the blazing light of Your love.

We will also be raised
to life as he was.

Romans 6:5 NLT

The Gift

April 12

God does not give me eternal life. He is eternal life! What He gives me is Himself. He comes to live inside of me.

Death no longer has any power over him.

Romans 6:9 NLT

He Is Strong!

April 13

I know what God wants me to do. It won't be easy. And the load will be heavy. But I can do it. I will not let it crush me. I will put one end on God's shoulders. He is strong. Together we will get it done.

Cast your burden
on the LORD.

Psalm 55:22

Squeezed

April 14

Sometimes it hurts. But I will not complain. Jesus loves me. And He is working to make something wonderful. But to get the juice, the grapes must be squeezed! I won't whine when I feel squeezed.

"Take My yoke upon you
and learn from Me."

Matthew 11:29

Does He?

April 15

What's the big deal? God doesn't care if I do that, does He? I'm sure it won't matter. Or will it? I don't really know. But I am His. And I'm not going to do it until I'm sure.

The heart of Asa was loyal
all his days.

2 Chronicles 15:17

Come On Down!

April 16

I feel great today! And I'd like to feel this way forever. But I can't. Sooner or later I will have to get up off my cloud and come down from the mountain. God is on the mountain. But He is in the valley as well.

"While you have the light, believe in the light."

John 12:36

Be God's

April 17

I am God's. I will get out of the boat. I will run to Him across the water. The water is deep. But He can do anything. He won't let me sink. He is calling. And I must go!

He put on his outer garment. . .
and plunged into the sea.

John 21:7

Ready or Not

April 18

I am ready, Lord. Ready to do something great and big and amazing. Ready to do something so small that no one will ever notice. Here I am. You can send me.

God called to him. . . .
And he said, "Here I am."

Exodus 3:4

Not to Me

April 19

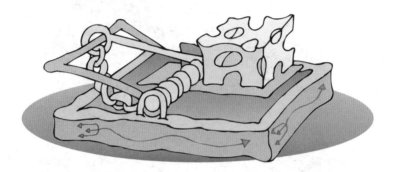

Many things will try to pull me away from God. Have I done something hard for Him? Good! But now I must watch out for the little things—the things that don't seem to matter. Sometimes they can be the most dangerous trap of all!

> For Joab had defected
> to Adonijah, though he had not
> defected to Absalom.
>
> 1 Kings 2:28

Worry!

April 20

Why am I worried? Why am I afraid? Why do I think that God will forget about me? O Lord, please forgive me! You have not forgotten me. But I have forgotten You.

For all the promises of God in Him are Yes, and in Him Amen.

2 Corinthians 1:20

Don't Hurt Him Now!

April 21

"What about this? What about that? First show me, and then I'll believe!" Am I hurting Jesus with the questions I ask? He loves me. He will take care of me. He is here.

"Have I been with you so long, and yet you have not known Me, Philip?"

John 14:9

Good-bye
April 22

I miss my friend. She meant so much to me. She showed me how to be like Jesus. And now she is gone. But God meant for her to go. God doesn't want me to trust in my friend. He wants me to trust in Him.

All of us who have had that veil removed can see and reflect the glory of the Lord.

2 Corinthians 3:18 NLT

Worship and Work

April 23

Here are my hands, Lord. Use them to make something beautiful. And here is my heart, too. Help me to fall in love with You. Help me not to love the good things I do more than I love You.

For we are God's fellow workers.

1 Corinthians 3:9

What to Want

April 24

I can work hard. I can do a good job. People will like what I do. But God does not want me to care what people think. He wants me to love them. He wants me to show someone else the way home to Him.

"Nevertheless do not rejoice
in this, that the spirits
are subject to you."

Luke 10:20

In the Mood

April 25

I'm just not in the mood right now. I know what I need to do. And I don't really want to do it. But I will do it. God gave me His best. So I will give Him my best. Even when I feel like I do today.

> Be ready in season
> and out of season.
>
> 2 Timothy 4:2

Abraham Trusted God

April 26

Abraham loved God. He was ready to do anything God asked. Even if it meant going against everything he had come to believe. Beliefs can be wrong. Abraham did not trust his beliefs. Abraham trusted God.

"Take now your son. . . ."

Genesis 22:2

What Do I Want?

April 27

I want to do great things. And God may let me. But great things come and great things go. Sometimes they're just an accident. God never gives me anything by accident. God gave me Jesus. But do I want Him?

"Do you seek great things
for yourself?"

Jeremiah 45:5

What I Will Get

April 28

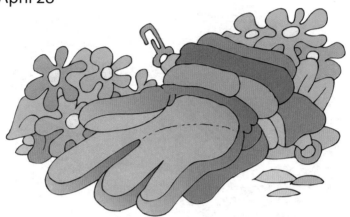

God is greater than the greatest thing I will ever do. He is more valuable than any good thing that will ever be put into my hands. I will stop worrying so much about things. I will give Jesus my heart.

"I will give your life to you as a prize in all places, wherever you go."

Jeremiah 45:5

Un-Certainly!

April 29

Who knows what will happen today? God knows! God knows what to do. God knows which way to go. God knows. And He loves me. I will trust Him and take the next step.

It has not yet been revealed what we shall be.

1 John 3:2

Real Love

April 30

I can love. I don't have to hate. I don't have to get angry. God's love is flowing through me like a wild river. I forget to love. I get filled up with selfishness. But when I open my heart, God's river of love comes pouring into me. At last I can love.

Love suffers long
and is kind.

1 Corinthians 13:4

Lights, Camera. . .

May 1

In my heart I want to do good. And with that very same heart I long for people to notice me. That is not right. I am not an angel. I am just a child. A child God can use. Even if no one is looking.

For we walk by faith,
not by sight.

2 Corinthians 5:7

Patience

May 2

I can wait. God is faithful. He will do what He says He will do!

"Though it tarries,
wait for it."

Habakkuk 2:3

Pray for Her!

May 3

I will pray for her. I will pray that God will change her heart. And if God has to break her heart to change it, I will let Him. I won't get in the way. I won't try to help. If I let Him, God will do something beautiful.

Never stop praying, especially for others. Always pray by the power of the Spirit.

Ephesians 6:18 CEV

Pray for Him!

May 4

Sometimes I want my own way. I want God to do what I want. I want Him to make people act the way I want them to. I need to stop being so stubborn. I need to be more like Jesus.

We can boldly enter
heaven's Most Holy Place
because of the blood of Jesus.

Hebrews 10:19 NLT

Tell Him!

May 5

I will tell him about Jesus. I don't need to change his mind. I don't need to point out every little sin. The love of God's Holy Spirit will do all that. But first I must tell him that Jesus loves him.

For the time has come
for judgment to begin
at the house of God.

1 Peter 4:17

Tell Her!

May 6

I will tell her about Jesus. She may not like it. She may not want to hear. But God was patient with me. So I will be patient with her. I will tell her. God will bring her home.

Stand fast therefore
in the liberty by which
Christ has made us free.

Galatians 5:1

This Old House

May 7

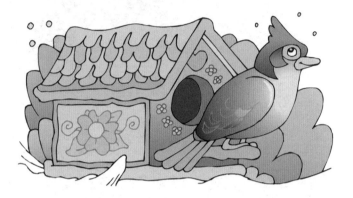

What am I building? And whose idea was it? One day God will inspect my work. If it was done His way, it will be allowed to stand. But if it was not—if I never asked God what He wanted—it will have to be knocked down.

"Sit down first and count the cost."

Luke 14:28

Ready, Aim. . .

May 8

I am like a bow and arrow in God's hands.
God stretches and pulls. At times I feel like
I will break. But God does not stop. He keeps
on stretching. God can see the target. He will
hit it. When He is ready I will fly!

"Because you have kept
My command to persevere. . ."

Revelation 3:10

Don't Lose Your Vision

May 9

God is alive in everything I do. He's in the great big important things. He's in the little things, too. I can trust Him when my work is easy. And I can trust Him when the goal looks like it's still a million miles away.

Where there is no revelation, the people cast off restraint.

Proverbs 29:18

Just Do It!

May 10

I know what God wants. So I'm going to get up and do it. I won't put it off. I won't be afraid. I won't wonder, or worry, or look for God to give me a special message. I will trust Him. I will do it!

Add to your faith virtue.

2 Peter 1:5

Him!

May 11

God, I can't love him. He's selfish and mean.
Just like I was. Just like I am. But You love me
anyway. Your love changed my heart. It can
change his, too. So I will love him. Just like
You loved me.

Add to your. . .
brotherly kindness love.

2 Peter 1:5, 7

Having No Habits

May 12

God does not want to give me good habits. God wants to change my heart. My good habits shout, "Look at me!" I may pay more attention to my good habits than I do to God. God wants me to look only at Him. He wants to put Jesus in place of my habits.

If all these things are in you and are growing, they will help you to be useful and productive in your knowledge of our Lord Jesus Christ.

2 Peter 1:8 NCV

Easy Does It

May 13

God's gentle voice is whispering in my ear. He is showing me the right thing to do. I will listen when God speaks. His commands are easy to keep. All I have to do is say, "Okay!"

"I always try to do what I believe is right before God and people."

Acts 24:16 NCV

Even Here

May 14

I don't like this very much. In fact, I don't like it at all. But here I am. God put me here for a reason. I will let His tender love pour out of my heart—even here.

. . .so that the life of Jesus may also be seen in our bodies.

2 Corinthians 4:10 NLT

Powerhouse!

May 15

I will give away what God has given me! God put His love in my heart. Now I must give it away to someone else. I must let His love pour back out through my hands and my feet and my heart and my mouth.

. . .that you may know
what is the hope of His calling.

Ephesians 1:18

Everything I Need

May 16

God loves me. He knows what I need. Every star in the sky lights the night with His love. He made each tiny grain of sand. God knows where I am. God hears when I pray. He will give me everything I need.

These are the promises that enable you to share his divine nature.

2 Peter 1:4 NLT

Son of Man

May 17

How much does Jesus love me? He loves me so much He became a man. He stepped out of heaven. He stepped into a human body! He gave up being with God to become like me. And because He did, one day I will step out of my body and step into heaven with Him.

He left them
and was taken up
into heaven.

Luke 24:51 NIV

Consider the Lilies

May 18

Birds do not worry. Stars don't get upset. Lilies don't hurry from this thing to that. But every last one is alive with God's love. I don't need to be useful. I just need to be His!

"Consider the lilies
of the field."

Matthew 6:28

Together

May 19

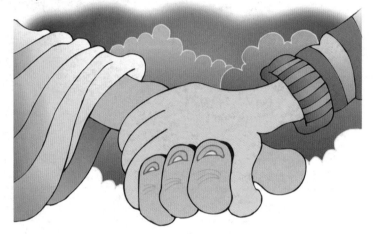

Trouble will come. But I will not be afraid. God is here. He is bigger than any trouble. Nothing will ever separate me from His love. My hand is in His. We will go through this together. And we will reach the other side of the trouble.

Who shall separate us from the love of Christ?

Romans 8:35

I Can Do All Things

May 20

I can do it—I know I can! Jesus is alive inside my heart. I will never say, "I can't." "I can't" just means "I won't." Sometimes I feel so grumpy or sad or lazy. But no matter how I feel, Jesus says I can do all things—when I trust in Him!

"Stand firm,
and you will win life."

Luke 21:19 NIV

Everything

May 21

Why should I worry? Jesus loves me. He will give me everything I need. I won't waste my time worrying about how to get more things. I don't need more things. I need Jesus.

"But seek first the kingdom of God. . . ."

Matthew 6:33

Why?

May 22

Why do I feel so lonely? What is God doing?
God is answering prayer! Jesus prayed that
I would be one with the Father just like He is.
And now God is answering His prayer. He is
letting me feel lonely so I will go closer to Him.

". . .that they all
may be one."

John 17:21

Careful Now!

May 23

I can be very careful. I can worry over every little thing. I can grumble and groan over every last wee, teeny, tiny, small thing. Or I can trust in Him.

"Do not worry about your life."

Matthew 6:25

Fall Down, Go Boom

May 24

O God, I have made so many mistakes. I want to be good. I want to do the right thing. Why can't I do it? Why is it so hard? Over and over again I fail. But You reach out Your hand. You take me in Your arms. Your tender love melts my fear away. O God, You are so big. And I am so small. Please forgive me. I want to be like You.

And when I saw Him,
I fell at His feet as dead.

Revelation 1:17

Very Interesting

Look at all these beautiful things! Every one of them is good. And every one has come from God. But which one should I choose? I just don't know! So I will pray. And I will listen. God will show me what to do.

"If you take the left, then I will go to the right. . ."

Genesis 13:9

Don't Stop Now!

May 26

Jesus said pray—and never stop! So that's just what I will do. I will tell Him every good thing that makes me happy. I will tell Him every sad thing that breaks my heart. He wants to hear me. He wants to listen. So I will tell Him! Twenty-four hours every day—anytime, anywhere, anything, any way! I will never, ever, ever stop. I will pray!

Pray without ceasing.

1 Thessalonians 5:17

He Is Here

May 27

Jesus is here. His Holy Spirit is alive deep inside my heart. He will teach me right from wrong. He will hold me when I am afraid. He is never far away. Right now—right this very minute— Jesus is here!

". . .clothed with power from on high."

Luke 24:49 NIV

No Doubt about It

May 28

Jesus knows what to do. Everything will be okay. I don't need to ask questions. I don't need to know the reason why. I am His. He is here. Everything will be okay.

"At that time
you won't need to ask me for anything."

John 16:23 NLT

In Jesus' Name

May 29

Jesus' name is not a magic word that I use to get everything I want. But when I am truly His—when my heart and mind and everything I want belong to Him—I can ask God for anything. And He will do it!

> "In that day you will ask
> in My name."
>
> John 16:26

Yes, But. . .

May 30

I want to follow Jesus. But what if He asks me to do something crazy? What will I do then? I will trust Him. I will risk everything and do what God says. When He asks me to jump out in faith, I will trust Him. I know He will catch me.

"Lord, I will follow You, but. . ."

Luke 9:61

What God Can Do

May 31

People will hurt me. But I won't let that make me mad. I know what God's love can do. His love can melt the coldest heart. It can change anyone! It can even change me.

Jesus did not commit Himself
to them. . .for He knew
what was in man.

John 2:24–25

But What about Him?

But what about him? Can God save him?
Can his tangled-up heart be made new? God
knows! God has done it before. He did it for
me. And I know God will do it again.

"Son of man,
can these bones live?"

Ezekiel 37:3

Haunted—by God!

June 2

God wants to haunt me! He wants to fill up every attic and closet and basement in my heart until nothing else can get inside. No worries. No cares. No shadows or fears. His Spirit scared them all away. Haunt me, Jesus!

Who is the man
that fears the LORD?

Psalm 25:12

Secret Joy

June 3

Who is my true friend? The one who shares her hurts? Maybe. But anyone can do that. And just about anyone will. A true friend longs to share her secret joy. God's secret joy is Jesus. He shares Jesus with me. And now Jesus' secret joy is me.

The secret of the LORD
is with those who fear Him.

Psalm 25:14

Never Ever

June 4

Jesus said He would never leave me. He said He would never stop loving me. And not one of my sinful, foolish mistakes will ever make Him change His mind.

"I will never leave you nor forsake you."

Hebrews 13:5

Fear Not!

June 5

God wants me to say what He says. And I can trust everything that God says. Am I afraid? I will remember the Bible. And the Bible says, "Fear not!"

He Himself has said. . .
So we may boldly say. . .

Hebrews 13:5–6

Work It Out

June 6

I will "work out" what God has "worked in." Jesus changed my heart. But do my words and my deeds shine with the light of His love? I won't always do the right thing. And sometimes I won't even want to. But God is inside me, helping me.

Work out your own salvation.

Philippians 2:12

My One True Love

June 7

What is the most important thing in my life? Is it a person? A thing? When I make Jesus my one true love, everything else will bloom and grow just the way it should.

"If you ask anything in My name, I will do it."

John 14:14

Ship Ahoy!

June 8

My life is like a little boat anchored in the harbor. The water is calm and smooth. The breeze is gentle and warm. And I am safe. But I cannot stay here forever. God wants me to launch out into the wild, open water; to ride the mighty, crashing waves. He wants me to let go. He wants me to trust Him and follow Him wherever He may go.

"If you know these things, blessed are you if you do them."

John 13:17

Poor in Spirit

June 9

My heart is like a poor, hungry beggar. Without Jesus my heart is empty. But I won't be ashamed to beg. Jesus loves poor beggars. The kingdom of heaven belongs to them!

"For everyone who asks receives."

Luke 11:10

Knock, Knock!

June 10

Jesus said, "Knock and I will open the door. Ask and you will receive." But what am I asking for? Do I really need more new things? Or do I need Jesus to come into my heart—and make everything new?

"Seek, and you will find."

Luke 11:9

Come to Me

June 11

O God, what should I do? I don't want to be selfish anymore. But I don't know how to stop! Did Jesus say, "Stop"? No! Jesus said, "Come!" I will stop trying to stop. I will run into His arms. Look out, Jesus. Here I come!

"Come to Me."

Matthew 11:28

Just the Chicken Pox?

June 12

Jesus wants me to be like Him. Does all of me look like Jesus? Or am I still selfish sometimes? Am I all speckled with little selfish spots, as though I had the chicken pox? Jesus wants to heal all of me. If I follow Him, He will make me like Him.

"Rabbi. . .where are You staying?" . . . "Come and see."

John 1:38–39

Not for Me to Say

June 13

Jesus wants me to follow Him. He wants me to act like Him. It's not my job to tell other people how they should act. I just have to follow Jesus. Then they will see Him in me.

"Follow Me."

Mark 1:17

It's Not about Me

June 14

I can trust God. My heart does not have to be a junk drawer full of worries and doubts. In every big, scary thing—in every little, ordinary thing—I can trust Him. I don't have to be afraid.

"Abide in Me."

John 15:4

No Big Thing

June 15

Jesus did big things. And I want to do big things, too. But I don't need to be a star. I can pour out God's love in a million little ways. Jesus did amazing miracles. But He knelt down and washed dirty feet as well. I will do little loving things, too.

But also. . .add. . .

2 Peter 1:5

Taste and See

June 16

My life won't always shine. Jesus' life didn't shine all the time either. But He always followed God. He was always loving. Every day, even.

"Greater love has no one than this, than to lay down one's life for his friends."

John 15:13

Don't
June 17

Do I like to point out other people's faults? Jesus says, "Don't." God can do that without hurting. But I am not God. When I point out every tiny little thing that is wrong with my friend, I can be sure that there is still a great big ugly thing wrong with me.

"Judge not, that you
be not judged"

Matthew 7:1

Just Don't Look Down

June 18

Peter walked on the water. The waves were crashing. The wind was howling. But Peter didn't see the waves. He didn't feel the wind. All he saw was Jesus. I can do anything God wants—if I will keep my eyes on Him.

But when Peter saw the wind and the waves, he became afraid.

Matthew 14:30 NCV

It's All for Ewe

June 19

Jesus wants me to feed His sheep. His "sheep" are everywhere. I can feed them by being kind and loving. I don't have to make people act the way I think they should. I just have to love them.

"Do you love Me? . . .
Feed My sheep."

John 21:17

When to Say When

June 20

I will pray for my friend. She needs to know that Jesus loves her. Jesus wants to help her. I will not wait until later. He wants me to pray for her. I will do it now. I will stop worrying so much about my own problems. I will pray.

And the LORD restored Job's losses when he prayed for his friends.

Job 42:10

Keep It Simple

June 21

I will stop worrying about me. I will get down on my knees. I will pray for others. I will stop thinking about me so much.

> But you are. . .
> a royal priesthood.
>
> 1 Peter 2:9

A Tough Test

June 22

My friend can be pushy and selfish. But why does it bother me? Is it because he should know better? Or because those very same things live in my heart, too? God forgives me. So I can forgive my friend.

"For in the same way you judge others, you will be judged"

Matthew 7:2 NIV

Jesus Rules!

June 23

Who is the king of my heart? Is it Jesus? Or is it sin? My heart cannot serve two kings. When I'm selfish, I make sin the king instead of God. I kill God's life in me. I don't want to make God sad. I want God to be my King.

. . .a Man of sorrows
and acquainted with grief.

Isaiah 53:3

It Is Sin

June 24

There is something wrong with me. It is sin.
It's not my temper or my personality—I have
sinned. That means I am selfish. I believe I'm
the center of the world. Nothing can make me
better—nothing but the blood of Jesus Christ.

"This is your hour,
and the power of darkness."

Luke 22:53

Make It Through

June 25

It's okay to cry. Bad things happen. God did not make a mistake. He did not stop loving me. He is working for my good, even though I can't understand. God is here. And we will make it through.

"What shall I say? 'Father, save Me from this hour'?"

John 12:27–28

New Every Morning

June 26

Jesus is ready to help me. He is ready right now. He knows what I need. He wants me to have it. His well of love will never run dry. Yesterday's help is all used up. I need Him right now. So I will go and get my bucket. I will fill my bucket from the deep well of Jesus' love. And then I will pray!

As God's co-workers
we urge you not to receive
God's grace in vain.

2 Corinthians 6:1 NIV

Don't Lean on That

June 27

What am I leaning on? Is it wobbly and weak?
Or is it steady and strong? When I lean on Jesus,
I will stand. But if I begin to lean on my ways
and my plans and all of my things instead of
leaning on Jesus, my things will break! And
I will fall down.

"I am with you to deliver you,"
says the LORD.

Jeremiah 1:8

Gotcha!

June 28

Jesus has me. I am His! I will talk about the good things He does. I will share His Word with tender love. The Word of God will bring new life. But first it must flow clean and pure in me.

Christ has taken hold of me.

Philippians 3:12 CEV

Cut It Off
June 29

I just can't do that anymore. I used to do it all the time. It never bothered me one bit. And my friends still do it. But now I know it breaks God's heart. It's like a black, rotten spot on the apple of my life. And I am the apple of His eye. So I will cut off anything that makes a spot on my life's apple.

"If your right hand causes you to sin. . ."

Matthew 5:30

Do It Now

June 30

Am I mad at my friend? Jesus says, "Forgive!" But I was right and she was wrong! It doesn't matter. Jesus says, "Forgive her." He says, "Make it right." He says, "Do it now."

"Agree with your adversary quickly."

Matthew 5:25

You're under Arrest

July 1

I was wrong. Jesus asked me to forgive. But I would not. So God arrested me! He put my heart in prison. And now there can be no escape—not until I forgive—not until I make it right—not until I let Him change my heart. Please change my heart, Jesus.

"You will by no means get out of there till you have paid the last penny."

Matthew 5:26

I Can't Do That

July 2

She is my very best friend. And we always do everything together! But now she wants me to do something wrong—something that will break God's heart! I love her very much. But I can't do that. My heart belongs to Him.

You cannot be my disciple,
unless you love me more than
you love. . .your own life.

Luke 14:26 CEV

Put It There

July 3

O Lord, please help me. I keep making the same mistake over and over again. I want to change. I know this is wrong. Take my selfishness. Burn it with the fire of Your love. I know it will hurt. But I want to be filled with love.

"Woe is me, for I am undone!
Because I am a man of unclean lips."

Isaiah 6:5

Don't Worry about It

July 4

Oh, silly me! There I go again, worrying about what might happen. God will work it all out. But I worry He won't work it out the way I want. I don't need to have my own way though. When I open my heart to God's way, all my worries go away.

Do not fret—it only causes harm.

Psalm 37:8

Count on God

July 5

I can count on God. When trouble comes,
God will be with me. When good things come,
He will be there, too. So when I make plans, I'll
always remember—no matter what happens,
God will be there.

Commit your way to the LORD. . .
and He shall bring it to pass.

Psalm 37:5

Dream Come True

July 6

I have a dream. And God will make that dream come true, because my life is His. My dreams are His, too—His to shape and mold into anything He wants. So I will let God shape my dreams. They are in good hands. He is making something beautiful.

The parched ground shall become a pool.

Isaiah 35:7

Exactly Like Him

July 7

It's not always easy to do the right thing. And thank God it's not! Following Jesus is good exercise. It makes me work hard. But Jesus is changing my heart. And He will not stop until I am exactly like Him. He loves me.

"Narrow is the gate and difficult is the way which leads to life."

Matthew 7:14

I Will

July 8

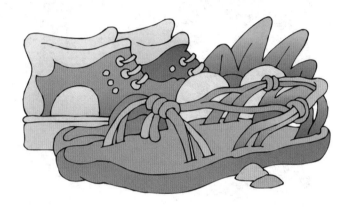

I want to follow Jesus. But where will He lead me?
I don't really know. But I do know He loves me.
And He will be there, no matter what happens.
So I won't be afraid. I will serve the Lord!

"Choose for yourselves this day
whom you will serve."

Joshua 24:15

Who, Me?

July 9

Surely God doesn't want me to do this! I'm too weak and too small. I'm not good enough. But God does want me to do this hard thing. And the weaker and more helpless I am, the better! God isn't looking for someone with something. He's looking for someone with nothing— nothing but His Son, Jesus.

"You cannot serve the LORD."

Joshua 24:19

Time to Wake Up

July 10

Jesus loves me. He wants me to be happy. But He doesn't want me to be lazy. Jesus wants to stir up my sleepy heart. He wants me to get busy. He wants me to go out and share His love with my friends.

Stir up love and good works.

Hebrews 10:24

That I May Know Him

July 11

I want to know Jesus. I want to serve Him. But I don't want to get mixed up. I don't want to think that the good things I do are more important than Jesus. I don't want to look at the good things I do. I just want to look at Jesus.

. . .that I may know Him.

Philippians 3:10

Body Building

July 12

Jesus wants me to build up His Body. Everyone in the world who loves Jesus is part of His Body. Jesus' Body needs me to do my part. I need to care about others, not just myself. Then I will be a Body builder!

. . .until we are all joined together in the same faith and in the same knowledge of the Son of God.

Ephesians 4:13 NCV

Good-bye, Old Friend

July 13

My friend moved away. I had to say good-bye to him. Oh, how I miss him. My heart feels empty without him. But now I have more room in my heart for Jesus. Jesus will fill the empty space with His love.

In the year that King Uzziah died, I saw the Lord.

Isaiah 6:1

Coward!

July 14

He hurt me. And now I want to hurt him back! But I must not. That would hurt Jesus. I am not a coward. I am someone who follows Jesus. So I will forgive. And I will turn the other cheek.

"But whoever slaps you on your right cheek, turn the other to him also."

Matthew 5:39

IOU

July 15

I owe everything to Jesus. So I will let Him change my heart. I will let Him pour His love out through me. Here I am, Lord. Take me where You will. My heart belongs to You.

I must tell the good news to everyone.

Romans 1:14 CEV

He Won't Forget

July 16

I'm not sure what to do. But I'm not going to worry about it. Why should I worry? God is my Father. He loves me. I won't ever think of anything that He will forget!

"How much more will your Father. . .give good things to those who ask Him!"

Matthew 7:11

I Can't See You!

July 17

Do I want people to like me? Do I want them to see how good I am? That seems like a good thing. But when people look at me—they can't see Jesus. The cure for this problem is very simple. Jesus wants me to give up trying to impress everyone. Right now.

When I came to you,
I did not come with eloquence
or human wisdom.

1 Corinthians 2:1 NIV

My Master

July 18

Many people would like to tell me what to do. They would like to see me do things that would break God's heart. But I will not listen to them. And I don't have to! My heart listens to only one Person. And His name is Jesus Christ.

And he said,
"Who are You, Lord?"

Acts 9:5

You Are Worthy

July 19

God will not force me to obey. If He did, He would be like a mean teacher who didn't care about me. But when I see God for who He is—when I feel His love in my heart—what can I say but "Yes, Lord, I will do whatever You say"?

"You call Me Teacher and Lord, and you say well, for so I am."

John 13:13

Treasure

July 20

There are times when God will do amazing things. And that is very exciting. But I must never allow the excitement of what God can do steal away the treasure of who He is. He loves me!

Those who wait on the Lord. . .
shall walk and not faint.

Isaiah 40:31

Blessed Like This

July 21

I've tried so hard to be good. I've tried to do what Jesus says. But I just can't do it! Is God mad at me? No! I have been blessed! Jesus says, "Stop trying to be good. Let Me come inside. Now I can change your heart."

"Blessed are the poor in spirit."

Matthew 5:3

Saints and Children

July 22

I am a good friend. I like to help. My parents are proud of me. I want to grow up to be someone special. And that's good. But God wants something different. He wants me! He wants to make my heart His home.

God's will
is for you to be holy.

1 Thessalonians 4:3 NLT

It's Mine

July 23

Everything God has is mine. His goodness. His love. His holiness. His faith. Everything! He gave them all to me. Because I deserve it? No. Because He loves me.

He sent Christ Jesus
to save us and to make us
wise, acceptable, and holy.

1 Corinthians 1:30 CEV

To Be or Not to Be

July 24

Jesus wants me to do the right thing. But He wants me to *be* the right thing even more. God sees all the good things I do. But why do I do them? Jesus wants my reasons to be as clean and pure as He is.

"Unless your righteousness exceeds the righteousness of the scribes. . ."

Matthew 5:20

Dynamite

July 25

God's Word is like dynamite! It will explode everything in my heart that was not built by Jesus. I don't always understand God's Word. But when I am still—and when I listen with my heart—*kaboom!* God's Spirit blows away the darkness and I can see.

"Blessed are. . ."

Matthew 5:3

Pure in Heart

July 26

God knows my heart. He knows about the good things that live there. He knows about the bad things, too. I don't have to pretend there are no bad things. God can fix the bad things. But first I must give Him my heart.

Out of your heart come. . .

Matthew 15:19 CEV

The Way to Know

July 27

Do I want to know what the Bible means?
Then I must do what the Bible says. Do I feel
a little confused about what God wants? Then
there must be something I don't want to obey!
Maybe I don't want to share. Maybe I don't want
to forgive someone. If I let Him, God's Spirit will
show me what to do.

"If people choose to do
what God wants, they will know
that my teaching comes from God."

John 7:17 NCV

What Is God's Goal?

July 28

I did just what God said. And now He has to make me a big success. Right? Maybe. But God's goal is not my success. That is my goal. God's goal is that I trust Him and treat peple right as I try to do His will.

He made His disciples get into the boat and go before Him to the other side.

Mark 6:45

They Came with Him!

July 29

The sky is dark with angry clouds. Did God go away? No! *The clouds are a sign that He is here.* Without them I would have no faith—no faith that God can blow clouds away. And when He does, clean bright light will shine in my heart.

Behold, He is coming
with clouds.

Revelation 1:7

Just an Illusion

July 30

I thought she would help. I thought she cared.
She was my one true friend. How could she do
that to me? At first I was hurt. But now I see.
God doesn't want me to give my heart to
anyone but Jesus. And when my heart
belongs to Him, no one else can hurt me.

Jesus did not commit Himself
to them. . .for He knew
what was in man.

John 2:24–25

Sloppy Joe
July 31

Jesus loves me—mistakes and all. But He is not about to leave me that way! God says, "Tuck those in! Button that up!" He will finish what He started. And my heart will be beautiful.

Let patience have
its perfect work.

James 1:4

Did I Go?

August 1

God said, "Go." But did I go? Or did I worry about myself? My friend needs to know about Jesus. I will not keep God's love locked up inside. I will give it all away. I will go.

He departed from there
to teach and to preach
in their cities.

Matthew 11:1

Strength!

August 2

Trouble will come. But I am not afraid.
God is bigger than any trouble. I can turn and
face my fear. I can look it in the eye. Jesus says,
"Stand and fight." Where has my fear gone?
When I gave it to Jesus, it turned into something
else. The thing that used to make me weak
now makes me strong.

"Be of good cheer,
I have overcome the world."

John 16:33

Big God

August 3

God picked me. He has a plan for my life. We will go many places. Together we will do wonderful things. But His plan is much bigger than places or things. I cannot see it just now. But in my heart I hear it calling. I hear it calling me to Him!

"Behold, we are going up
to Jerusalem."

Luke 18:31

Brave God

August 4

Who can God use? That's easy. God can use anyone—anyone who puts God first. My friendship with God is the most important thing in my life.

Then He took
the twelve aside.

Luke 18:31

What Is God Doing?

August 5

Why did this happen? What is God doing?
I don't know. But God knows. And I can relax
and trust Him. God sees what I do not. He is
using this to make something beautiful.

But they understood
none of these things.

Luke 18:34

Why to Pray

August 6

God knows my heart. He knows just what I need. Before I even think to ask, His answer is already on the way. Jesus longs to hear my voice. Jesus died to set me free. Oh, how He loves me. I will talk to Him.

"In that day you will ask
in My name."

John 16:26

In My Father's House

August 7

I want to live in my Father's house. I want to curl up in His arms. I want His heart to beat in mine. I want to listen to His gentle voice. O Lord, have Your way with me.

"Did you not know
that I must be about
My Father's business?"

Luke 2:49

Room for Him

August 8

God put His Son in me. And now Jesus is born again inside my heart. He will live there. He will grow there. When Mary gave birth to the baby Jesus, there was no room for Him in the inn. But this time there is plenty of room for His Spirit—right here in my heart!

"That Holy One who is to be born will be called the Son of God."

Luke 1:35

Simply Beautiful

August 9

Does God hear me when I pray? Of course He does! God will always hear the prayers of His Son. And His Son is alive and well—right here inside of my heart!

"Father, I thank You
that You have heard Me."

John 11:41

Nobody Knows

August 10

My friend is hurting. I want to help her. I just don't know what to say or do. I know she loves Jesus. So she is in good hands. There's no need to get in God's way. I will pray. Jesus will heal her broken heart.

If you are suffering
in a manner that pleases God. . .
trust your lives to the God who
created you, for he will never fail you.

1 Peter 4:19 NLT

This Must Come

August 11

I feel so lonely. I miss my old friend. Everywhere I go, I remember the things we used to do together. I can't stop thinking about my friend. But God wants me to think about Him. My friend trusted God. And I will, too.

So he saw him no more.

2 Kings 2:12

Rest
August 12

Did I hear the howling wind? Did I see the crashing waves? Did I feel the angry, rolling sea? No, I'm sorry. I must have missed it. I was here with Jesus. All I could see was Him.

"Why are you fearful,
O you of little faith?"

Matthew 8:26

Quiet Now

August 13

God's voice is gentle and still. And I must be quiet to hear it. Is God saying, "Stop"? Then I will stop. God does not have to shout. I am listening to Him.

Do not quench the Spirit.

1 Thessalonians 5:19 NIV

Let Him

August 14

Jesus loves me. And because He does, He will correct me when I am wrong. But I don't like to be corrected. I know God can make me into something beautiful. Do I love Him enough to let Him do it?

"Do not despise the chastening of the Lord."

Hebrews 12:5

Born Again

August 15

Who can be born again? I can! I can stop pretending that I am good. I can put away my sin and selfishness. Now Jesus can come in. Now His love can make my heart brand new.

"You must be born again."

John 3:7

Do I Know Him?

August 16

Do I ever wonder if Jesus can really do what people say He can? Do I doubt Him? Do I do what I want—or do I do what Jesus wants? All my doubts and selfish feelings will go away when I'm really friends with Jesus.

"He calls his own sheep by name."

John 10:3

Hard

August 17

Did Jesus ask me to do something hard? Does He want me to do what I don't want to do? Now God is searching my heart. He is making it clean and pure. He will not force me to do what He wants. But if I love Him, I will do what He wants me to do.

"Sell all that you have. . . and come, follow Me."

Luke 18:22

But How?

August 18

How can I do it? It's just too hard. Surely God doesn't want me to do that! But I am His. And everything I have is His, too. I will let Him shape me and use me any way He wants.

> But when he heard this,
> he became very sorrowful,
> for he was very rich.
>
> Luke 18:23

Straight to Jesus

August 19

God wants me to be whole and healthy in Jesus. Nothing should upset my friendship with Him. If anything comes between Him and me, I need to take care of it right away. Then I can go straight to Jesus.

"Come to Me."

Matthew 11:28

Peace—Be Still!

August 20

Has something come between Jesus and me?
Is it making me wobble and worry and fret?
I will tell God all about it. He will blow it far
away. He will put Jesus in its place.

"And I will give you rest."

Matthew 11:28

Poor in Spirit

August 21

Jesus loves me. I don't have to be strong or beautiful. I don't have to be important or useful or wise. I don't have to be anything at all. Here I am, Lord. Oh, how I love You.

"Blessed are
the poor in spirit."

Matthew 5:3

Good, Better, Best

August 22

Have I come to the end of my rope? Good! Am I just about ready to lose my grip? Even better! Did I let go and fall down? Best of all! At last I am lying at Jesus' feet. Now He can change my heart. He will fill me with the Holy Spirit.

"He will baptize you
with the Holy Spirit and fire."

Matthew 3:11

The Secret Place

August 23

Where is my secret place—the place where God can touch my heart—the place where we can be alone? That is where Jesus wants me to live. I will run to meet Him there.

"Pray to your Father who is in the secret place."

Matthew 6:6

I Forgot

August 24

Did God forget to answer my prayer? Or did I forget how to be loving and kind? I will ask God to forgive me. I will ask my friends to forgive me, too. Now when I pray, I know God will answer.

"What man. . .if his son asks for bread, will give him a stone?"

Matthew 7:9

Friends

August 25

Here is my heart, Lord. And here is my life, too. Please teach me how to love. Let me long to do Your will. Oh, how I love You. You are my friend.

"I have called you friends."

John 15:15

Am I Rubbing Him Out?

August 26

Do I worry and fret over every little thing? Worry is like an eraser. It rubs out God's face until I can't even see Him anymore. I will stop rubbing God out. God is not worried. I will trust Him. I will look up!

"Peace I leave with you,
My peace I give to you."

John 14:27

Make It Real

August 27

Did God show me what to do? Then I will do it! Did He tell me to forgive? Did He ask me to share His love? Did He show me the way to go? I will do it. I will make it real.

"Walk in the light while you can, so the darkness will not overtake you."

John 12:35 NLT

Teach Me to Pray

August 28

Why should I pray? Should I pray to get things? Should I pray to change things? Yes, I should! But what will I get? And what will God change? That's easy! I will get Jesus. And God will change me!

"Lord, teach us to pray."

Luke 11:1

Now It Is Mine

August 29

Do I trust God? Then He will test my faith. Can I believe Him when everything I see and hear tells me He is wrong? That is the test. Jesus says, "Trust Me and do not be afraid." When I trust Him, faith is mine!

"Did I not say to you
that if you would believe
you would see the glory of God?"

John 11:40

Wanted!

August 30

Did God use me? Good! I will thank Him. But I must never forget that God can use anyone. He can use a donkey. He can use a king! What really matters is that Jesus wants me. He loves me!

"Rejoice because your names are written in heaven."

Luke 10:20

Joy!
August 31

What is joy? Is it the happiness that comes from feeling good? Is it the excitement of doing what God wants? Or is it simply knowing that I am His—that Jesus loves me—and that He is alive right here inside of my heart?

". . .that My joy may remain in you, and that your joy may be full."

John 15:11

Holy

September 1

I am God's. My feet will follow where He leads.
My lips will speak His words of life. My thoughts
will flow clean, clear, and pure. Search my heart,
Lord. Burn up the things that make You sad.
I want to be like You.

"Be holy, for I am holy."

1 Peter 1:16

Open Up!

September 2

God doesn't care how good I act on the outside. He doesn't care how many nice things I have. He just wants me to be like Jesus. He doesn't want me to keep my life closed up like a bottle with the top on. He wants me to take the top off and pour myself out. He wants me to share myself.

"He who believes in Me. . .
out of his heart will flow rivers
of living water."

John 7:38

Pour It Out

September 3

Did God give me something good? If I keep it all to myself, it will turn sour. But if I pour it out as a gift to others, it will be as sweet to my friend as it was to me!

He would not drink it,
but poured it out to the LORD.

2 Samuel 23:16

His!

September 4

Who do I belong to? Do I belong to my mother? My father? My friends? Myself? Those people love me very much. And I love them. But my heart belongs to Jesus.

"They were Yours,
You gave them to Me."

John 17:6

In the Garden

September 5

When I was in trouble, Jesus came into the garden of my heart. He stayed with me until the terrible storm was past. Now Jesus wants me to come into the garden of His heart. He wants me to kneel down beside Him. We will pray together for my friends.

"Watch with Me."

Matthew 26:40

Love Like a River

September 6

God's love is like a mighty river. Is there something in its way? God's love will flow right around it—or wash it clean away!

". . .rivers of living water."

John 7:38

Pull Out the Plug

September 7

Is God's river of love flowing out of me? Or am I all plugged up? I will pull out the plug! I will give God my heart. I am not a cold, dead sea whose water can't flow out. I am a river of life— a river of God's life!

"The water I give them will become in them a spring of water welling up to eternal life."

John 4:14 NIV

All the Pieces

September 8

Jesus is alive inside my heart. And His love washed all my sins away. But something is wrong. My heart longs to hate when I have been hurt. I don't want to love someone so different from me. Did Jesus forget to fix these things? No! He wants me to leave them with Him. I have to give Him the parts of me that hate. I can't keep these things anymore. I have to let them go.

> . . .casting down. . .every high thing that exalts itself against the knowledge of God.
>
> 2 Corinthians 10:5

I Will!

September 9

I want to do many good things for God. But I want to obey Him most of all. Did I think of something good to do? I will tell God about it. And if He says, "Do it"—I will!

We take captive every thought to make it obedient to Christ.

2 Corinthians 10:5 NIV

Out in the Open

September 10

Do I spend time alone with God? Do I tell Him how I feel inside? Do I listen for His gentle voice? If I know Him here—in the quiet, secret place—then my heart will be quiet and happy even when noisy people are all around me.

"When you were under the fig tree, I saw you."

John 1:48

Sweet Feet

September 11

Where did God put me? What does He want me to do? Do I see a dirty foot? I will fill a bowl with water. I will go and find a towel. I will wash it nice and fresh and clean. I will do little, loving things for Jesus.

"You also ought to wash one another's feet."

John 13:14

Confused?

September 12

I don't understand why this is happening. And I'm not sure what to do. But I know that Jesus loves me. He is teaching me to trust Him. And the only way out of this mess is to go through it with Him.

"You do not know what you ask."

Matthew 20:22

I Surrender!

September 13

Jesus wants my heart. He wants it for His very own. He will not force me to give it to Him. He will never bargain or beg. Jesus is waiting. Will I give Him my heart?

"I have finished the work which You have given Me to do."

John 17:4

A Muddle Puddle

September 14

My heart is so confused I can't sleep at night. My poor mind is in a muddle! And what did all that worrying do? It got me twisted up in my covers! I'm so sorry, Lord. I'll stop worrying. If I just follow You, everything will be simple.

. . .the simplicity
that is in Christ.

2 Corinthians 11:3

Into the Light

September 15

Am I angry with my friend? I will drag that dark, angry feeling out into God's light. God will chase it far away. Now my heart is clean and pure.

We don't do shameful things
that must be kept secret.

2 Corinthians 4:2 CEV

Why God Hears

September 16

Does Jesus hear me when I pray? You bet He does! But why? Because I use the right words? Because I'm honest and sincere? No. I don't have to impress God. He hears me because He loves me. I'm His child!

"Pray to your Father who is in the secret place."

Matthew 6:6

That's Very Tempting

September 17

I'm not bad if I want to do something wrong. Everyone wants to do wrong things sometimes. But God helps me not to do the wrong thing. He wants me to lean on Him when I'm tempted to do wrong. I will do right if I turn away from wrong and turn to God.

The temptations in your life are no different from what others experience.

1 Corinthians 10:13 NLT

So Watch Out!

September 18

Satan will tempt me. He wants me to sin. Friends may want me to do bad things. But Satan wants something much worse than that! He wants me to stop loving and caring. He wants me to lose my friendship with Jesus.

We do not have a High Priest who cannot sympathize with our weaknesses.

Hebrews 4:15

Slip and Fall

September 19

I want to follow Jesus. But sometimes He leads me through hard things. Jesus faced troubles and temptations when He was on earth. Now He wants me to follow Him through my own troubles and temptations. If I follow Him, I won't slip and fall.

"But you are those who have continued with Me in My trials."

Luke 22:28

It's You I Like

September 20

Some people I like. And some I do not! I won't always like everyone I meet. But if my heart truly belongs to Jesus—if I'm walking in His light—He will show me how to love people—whether I like them or not!

"You shall be perfect,
just as your Father in heaven
is perfect."

Matthew 5:48

Forever

September 21

Who am I? Why am I here? That's easy! I am God's. God made me. And I am free. Free to worship Him and enjoy His love—forever!

Even before I was born,
the LORD God chose me
to serve him.

Isaiah 49:5 CEV

Yes, Master

September 22

Jesus will never force me to obey. Some days I wish He would. And some days I wish He'd just leave me alone. But God loves me too much to ever do that. He is teaching me to listen. He is teaching me to trust Him. He is teaching me to love.

"You call Me Teacher and Lord, and you say well, for so I am."

John 13:13

Growing Up

September 23

What do I want to be when I grow up? I'm not really sure. But I do know this: My plans may change. My dreams may change, too. But no matter what—I want to be God's.

"Behold, we are going up to Jerusalem."

Luke 18:31

Get Ready

September 24

God will use me. But how do I get ready?
I must let Jesus search my heart. Did He find
something I have been hiding? I will confess
my secret sin. I will give it all to Him. Every
day I will give Jesus my heart.

"First be reconciled
to your brother, and then come
and offer your gift."

Matthew 5:24

So Can I

September 25

Jesus wants me to do the impossible.
Did someone hurt my feelings? Jesus says,
"Forgive and then forget it ever happened."
But that's impossible! That's right! But He
will forget and forgive—and so can I.

"Whoever compels you to go
one mile, go with him two."

Matthew 5:41

Go Back

September 26

I am mad at her. And she is mad at me. Now I want to sing and give thanks to God. But Jesus says, "No." He says first I must forgive. But why me? That's easy! Jesus wants every last little part of me to be just like Him. So I must go back and make things right with her.

"If you. . .remember
that your brother
has something against you. . ."

Matthew 5:23

Peace and Joy

September 27

I love the Bible. It brings peace and joy. But sometimes it can hurt. Did God's Word find something in my heart that has to go? God loves me, but He wants to make me like Jesus. His love will shine on all my selfish darkness.

"Lord, I will follow You wherever You go."

Luke 9:57

Here's Looking at You

September 28

Jesus looked at me. He looked right into my heart! He saw my mistakes. He saw all my fears. He crumpled them up. He threw them all away. Now I can see Him! Oh, how He loves me. Now at last my heart is free!

"One thing you lack. . .
come, take up the cross,
and follow Me."

Mark 10:21

God Calling!

September 29

God has a plan for me. I don't know what it is right now. I don't know what I'll see or do. But one day I will hear Him call. And when I do, if I will answer yes, Jesus will do something amazing!

Woe is me
if I do not preach the gospel!

1 Corinthians 9:16

Bread and Wine

September 30

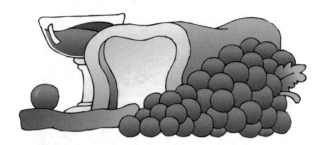

God wants to use me to help others. He wants to put His love inside me—and then He wants me to pour it out to my friends and family. When people have hungry hearts, He wants my life to feed them. Sometimes I want to keep everything all to myself. But God wants to use me. He wants to use me to help even the people I don't like.

I am glad when I suffer for you in my body, for I am participating in the sufferings of Christ.

Colossians 1:24 NLT

Going Up!

October 1

Jesus is alive inside of my heart. His love rides the dawn of the bright morning sun. He lifts me up to the mountaintops. I will run down the mountain. I will tell all my friends. I will help lift them up. Now they see Jesus, too.

Jesus took Peter, James, and John. . . up on a high mountain.

Mark 9:2

Coming Down

October 2

Yesterday God was so real and so close. Today He seems so far away. It's getting dark. And it's getting cold. But God is still here. He is right here in my heart.

"Have compassion on us
and help us."

Mark 9:22

Fight!

October 3

Has something come between Jesus and me? That thing will have to go! I will grab it by the arm. I will look it in the eye. I will tell it, "Go away!" I will get down on my knees and ask for God's help. And then I will fight until it's gone!

"This kind can come out by nothing but prayer and fasting."

Mark 9:29

I Am the Clay

October 4

Jesus is molding and shaping my heart.
At times His hands are tender and gentle. At
times He must press and squeeze and pound.
But I will let Him have His way. He is making
something beautiful. He is making me.

. . .called to be saints.

1 Corinthians 1:2

An Odd Couple

October 5

I can be neat and clean with each hair right in place, or rumpled and mussed like an unmade bed. God doesn't notice. That is not what matters. He is looking at my heart.

Adam sinned, and that sin brought death into the world. Now everyone has sinned. . .

Romans 5:12 CEV

I'd Be Happy To

October 6

I am not perfect. And it's beginning to look like I never will be! I know what to do. But I still make so many mistakes. I feel like I'm just no good. But God is faithful. I can open up my empty heart. God will fill it. He will fill it with His Son.

When it pleased God. . .
to reveal His Son in me. . .

Galatians 1:15–16

Be That Way

October 7

When I do something wrong, that is a sin.
And God wants me to do the right thing. But
He wants me to *be* the right thing even more.
Jesus forgives wrongdoing. But He died on
a cross so I could be right with Him.

He made Him
who knew no sin
to be sin for us.

2 Corinthians 5:21

I'm Listening Now

October 8

Am I listening for God's voice? Or am I listening for my own? I would love to do big things. And maybe I will. But is God really shouting, "Go and do big things"? Or is He simply whispering, "Come to Me"?

"Come to Me."

Matthew 11:28

On My Side
October 9

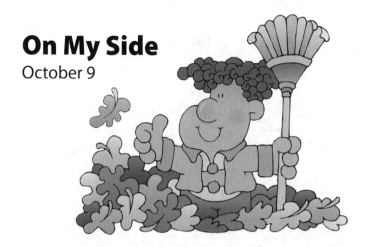

Did I obey God? Did I do what He said even though it was very hard? That's great! But God doesn't want me to be extra good just so people will look at me and think, *Wow! That kid is an angel*! No, God just wants me to stay close to Jesus. When Jesus and I are friends, He will always be on my side. And He will work things out for my good.

. . .instruments of righteousness to God.

Romans 6:13

Suddenly It's Mine

October 10

How can I know what the Bible really means?
I can study and search and think and be wise
and never understand. But when I get up and
do the things the Bible says to do—suddenly
it's mine!

"You have hidden these things
from the wise. . .and have
revealed them to babes."

Matthew 11:25

Silence

October 11

I prayed. And God heard me. But how do I know? He didn't say anything back. But God knows that I love Him. He knows He can trust me. I can trust Him, too. My heart is quiet. The answer will come.

He stayed two more days
in the place where He was.

John 11:6

Walk with God

October 12

I want to walk with God. But sometimes it's hard to keep up with Him! He does things so differently than I would. Is Jesus out ahead of me just now? I will run to catch up. I will do this His way. I want to walk with Him.

Enoch walked with God.

Genesis 5:24

Don't Look Now!

October 13

Where is God? Why doesn't He say anything? I wonder if my dreams will ever come true. I've been waiting so long. But I'm not going to give up now. Maybe God has to change a few things first. Maybe He has to change me. Then I can really love Him. And then He can use me to help the people around me.

He went out to his brethren and looked at their burdens.

Exodus 2:11

Tell Them

October 14

People all over the world need to hear about Jesus. And God wants me to tell them. But first He must be alive inside of my heart. When I grow up, God may send me across the world—or across the street! I will let Him decide. God is not my servant. I am His.

"Go. . .and make disciples
of all the nations."

Matthew 28:19

The Message

October 15

God is good. He is loving and kind. And He has done so much for me. Now I want to tell everyone! But what should I say? Should I talk about these things? Yes! But I must always remember this: God doesn't want people to be exactly like me. He wants them to be exactly like Jesus.

Christ is the sacrifice
that takes away our sins.

1 John 2:2 CEV

Keys, Please

October 16

I want to tell everyone about Jesus. And I would gladly work night and day to do it. But work is not the key to unlock the door to my friend's broken heart. The key to that is prayer!

"Pray the Lord of the harvest to send out laborers into His harvest."

Matthew 9:38

Greater Works

October 17

I want to do something great. I want to change the world! But here I am again, stuck right here in the same old place. What can I do today that really matters? What can I do to help? That's easy. I can pray!

"Greater works than these he will do, because I go to My Father."

John 14:12

True Devotion

October 18

Jesus said, "Do you love Me? Then feed My
sheep! Love what I love. Hate what I hate.
Trust Me when I've wandered off into the
morning mist. Don't worry about things.
Just be yourself. And love like I love You."

They went forth
for His name's sake.

3 John 7

Go, Dog, Go!
October 19

Hurry, hurry. Busy busy. Big, important things to do! No time for this. No time for that. I can't stop now. Too much to do! But why? Jesus is not in a hurry. So I'm not either. I think I'll spend some time with Him.

"My kingdom is not of this world."

John 18:36

Will I?

October 20

I want to be good. I want to do right. I want to learn how to be loving and kind. I want to let Jesus make His home in my heart. I want to do all of these things. But will I? Jesus will always love me—but only I can decide to let Him change my heart.

God's will
is for you to be holy.

1 Thessalonians 4:3 NLT

Walking on the Water

October 21

Peter got out of the boat. He walked across the water! That was an amazing miracle. Now Jesus wants me to do a miracle, too. He wants me to walk across my life today in a way that pleases Him.

. . .building yourselves up
on your most holy faith.

Jude 20

Man Overboard!

October 22

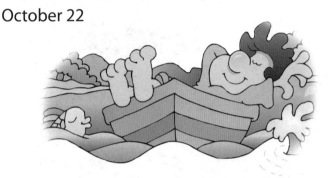

I've been holding on to my fears and worries as though they are life jackets to keep me safe. So why do I still feel scared and worried? Am I puzzled and confused? God will show me what to do. But when? When I pack up all my fears and doubts and fling them all overboard. Splash! Down they go. Now there's nothing left to keep me safe. Nothing but God's Holy Spirit.

The Spirit Himself
bears witness with our spirit.

Romans 8:16

Not a Bit of It

October 23

Do I hate someone—because of the color of her skin—or the way he talks—or because she acts differently than me? God does not. And He won't let me do it either. Do I own this secret sin? God will bring it into the light. He wants me to let Him wipe away all my hatred.

If anyone is in Christ,
he is a new creation;
old things have passed away.

2 Corinthians 5:17

Victory!

October 24

I'm fighting to do right. But I'm losing the war! I could struggle and strain to get the victory. But I think I'll run to Jesus instead. He will win the war. I will trust Him. And then I will be a sweet fragrance to Him!

Thanks be to God who always leads us in triumph in Christ.

2 Corinthians 2:14

Here and Now

October 25

Sometimes I think God could use me more
if I were older, if I lived somewhere else, if
I could do things better. But God wants to use
me right now, right here. He wants to be able
to say, "This is My child." Here and now, He has
a plan that's just for me.

I have become all things
to all men, that I might
by all means save some.

1 Corinthians 9:22

Who Is a Missionary?

October 26

A missionary is a person sent by God to teach His Word and share His love. But who is a missionary? That's easy. I am! And who will God send? That's right! He will send me.

"As the Father has sent Me, I also send you."

John 20:21

Way to Go

October 27

What is the best way to teach the Word of God? What is the best way to share His love? The best way to teach is to know God myself. The best way to share is to live for His love.

"Go therefore and make disciples of all the nations."

Matthew 28:19

It Is Finished

October 28

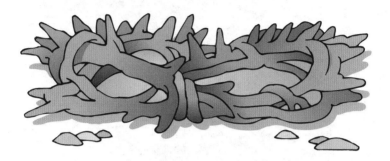

Why has God forgiven my sins? Because I'm sorry? Because I'm trying to do better? Because I promise to do what He says from now on? No. Jesus died on the cross. And my sins died there, too! How does it work? I don't really know. But it is true. And I do believe it. It is finished—my sins are already forgiven. I am saved!

Having been reconciled,
we shall be saved by His life.

Romans 5:10

All He Sees

October 29

Why did Jesus have to die? Jesus didn't do anything wrong! But God hung the sin of every person upon Him. When God looked at Jesus on the cross, all He saw was sin. And sin must be killed. So Jesus had to die. But Jesus has risen from the dead. He has risen right here inside of my heart. Now when God looks at me, He does not see my sin. All He sees is His living Son!

For God made Christ. . .to be the offering for our sin, so that we could be made right with God through Christ.

2 Corinthians 5:21 NLT

This Is Faith

October 30

Sometimes I feel silly following Jesus. Sometimes I think He asks me to do crazy things. But when I do every little thing for Jesus—no matter how silly—then I can see Him more and more. My faith isn't just in my head now. Now it's in my hands and feet. Now it is real.

Without faith
it is impossible to please Him.

Hebrews 11:6

Faith Is This

October 31

What will God give me when I learn to have faith? What will He do when I trust in His Word? God will give me Himself. He will make me His own. He will set me free.

". . .if you have faith as a mustard seed."

Matthew 17:20

Go with the Flow

November 1

Some days I like to be all by myself. But like my heart, this day is God's. Will I get to do what I want to today? Maybe. But God may have other plans. So I won't clog them up. I will go with the flow!

Do you not know that. . . you are not your own?

1 Corinthians 6:19

What to Keep

November 2

Should I do what God says? Should I keep His commands? What a silly question! Of course I should. I love God with all of my heart. Why would I listen to anyone else?

"If you love Me,
keep My commandments."

John 14:15

I Surrender

November 3

Part of me wants to do God's will. And part of me does not. Is God angry with me for feeling this way? No. Jesus loves me far too much to break in and steal my heart. He is waiting for me to give it to Him.

"I have been crucified with Christ."

Galatians 2:20

Do Something

November 4

God is calling me. Now it is up to me to go. I can't just sit here listening. I have to get up and do whatever He says. As soon as I do, He will come and meet me.

Draw near to God
and He will draw near to you.

James 4:8

Rejoice!

November 5

Why is this happening? What is God doing?
I knew just what I wanted. And then, splat! God
stepped on it. Just look at it. It's ruined! Now I'll
have to want something else. God wants what
is best for me.

> Be very glad—for these trials
> make you partners with Christ
> in his suffering.
>
> 1 Peter 4:13 NLT

Believe

November 6

I know what Jesus can do. I know He can heal people who are sick. I know He can feed people who are very hungry. I know He can bring a dead person to life. But can He do this for me? If I believe—He can!

"Do you believe this?"

John 11:26

They Make Me Mad!

November 7

Oh, these people! They make me so mad!
Why did God put me here? I'd like to run away!
But I must not. God did not put me here to run
away. He put me here to pray.

All things work together
for good to those who love God.

Romans 8:28

In God's House

November 8

I don't always know the right way to pray. But God knows. And when I don't know, He will pray for me. God's Holy Spirit will pray deep down inside my heart. *Shhh*! There He is. God's house is a house of prayer. And I am God's house. So this house will pray.

The Spirit prays for us in ways that cannot be put into words.

Romans 8:26 CEV

Lift Him Up

November 9

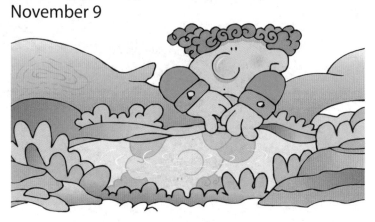

I want to tell the world about Jesus. But how should I do it? By being cute and funny? By being smart and telling good stories? How silly! Those things make people look at me. And no one will ever find Jesus if they're looking at me. I have to show them Jesus.

I now rejoice in my sufferings for you.

Colossians 1:24

Come Out and Play

November 10

The weather outside is cold and windy. And it's warm and cozy inside. But God is knocking on the door to my heart. Will I stay inside where it's safe and warm? Or will I put on my boots and go outside and play?

. . .fellow laborer
in the gospel of Christ.

1 Thessalonians 3:2

Like Abraham

November 11

Am I happy and content? I will thank God and enjoy His blessings. Is my heart broken and confused? I will trust God and walk alone with Him. He will lead me home.

"Take now your son."

Genesis 22:2

All Things Are New

November 12

Jesus changed my heart. He made every part of me brand new! I don't need to do bad things anymore. I don't even want to. The old me is gone. I am born again.

Old things have passed away;
behold, all things have become new.

2 Corinthians 5:17

Whom Do I Trust?

November 13

Whom do I trust? I trust Jesus. Not the story of Jesus. And not what someone has said about Him. But the real, live Son of God who took my sins away. I trust Him.

". . .the Son of God, who loved me and gave Himself for me."

Galatians 2:20

Are We There Yet?

November 14

Jesus will lead me. He knows what to do. He will look after everything. Big or small, it's all in His hands. I don't have to ask where we are going. I don't need to know if we're there yet. I can relax and trust in Him.

"As for me, the LORD has led me on the journey."

Genesis 24:27 NIV

It Isn't Easy

November 15

Sometimes I want to fix my friend's life.
I want to tell him how to act. I want to help
Jesus change him. But God wants me to get
out of His way. He wants me to look at Jesus
and wait for Him. And then Jesus will take
care of my friend.

"What is that to you?
You follow Me."

John 21:22

Halo There!

November 16

No one may notice me today. No one may say anything about the good things I do. That's okay. I'm not looking for a spotlight. I'm not trying to buy a halo. God knows where I am. That's good enough for me.

Whatever you do,
do all to the glory of God.

1 Corinthians 10:31

I Will Bless You

November 17

When Jesus says, "Come," I will come. When
He says, "Let go," I will let go. When He says,
"Trust Me," I will trust Him. When God speaks,
I will listen. "Now," God says, "I will bless you!"

"Because you have done this. . .
I will bless you."

Genesis 22:16–17

I Can—I Will!

November 18

Jesus will not do everything for me. He wants me to do some things myself. Did He ask me to stop doing that very bad thing? I won't say, "I can't." I can—and I will.

"If the Son makes you free, you shall be free indeed."

John 8:36

He Can—He Will!

November 19

I have sinned. I broke God's heart. How can He ever forgive me now? Sin must be punished! But God did not punish me. He punished Jesus instead. His death was the punishment for my sin. Oh, how God loves me. Now He can forgive me.

"When He has come,
He will convict the world of sin."

John 16:8

I Forgive You
November 20

God is love. He is gentle and kind. He has forgiven all of my sins. Not because He loved me, but because Jesus died. God's forgiveness cost Him His Son.

In Him we have. . .
the forgiveness of sins.

Ephesians 1:7

Come and Get It!

November 21

Jesus hates sin. He hates the terrible thing it does to my heart. He hates how it hangs on and will not let go. He hates it so much that He died to destroy it. And destroy it He did! It is finished. My heart is free.

"I have finished the work which You have given Me to do."

John 17:4

Off the Deep End

November 22

The ocean is beautiful and deep. But the way to the deepest, most wonderful part begins by getting my feet wet on the shore. I don't understand everything about God. And there's no need to pretend that I do. But I hear His voice. He is calling my name. And step by step He will lead me out into the deep—until at last I'm home with Him.

Whatever you do,
do all to the glory of God.

1 Corinthians 10:31

Wrong, Wrong, Wrong

November 23

My friend is wrong. Wrong, wrong, wrong!
Why can't she see it? Why won't she change?
I've got to do something. But what should I do?
Should I tell her about it? Should I try to set her
straight? No! I should pray for her.

Have mercy on us,
O Lord.

Psalm 123:3

I've Sprung a Leak!

November 24

Help! I've sprung a leak in my faith! I'm not sure that God loves me! I'm not sure I can trust Him! I'm not sure that He's leading in just the right way! Oh, look. Here's the problem. My eyes aren't on Jesus. But I can fix that! Now I can see Him. Now my faith's not leaking. Now He can fill me up right to the top!

Our eyes look to the LORD
our God.

Psalm 123:2

Deep Roots

November 25

Seasons will change. Friends will come and go. But one thing will always stay the same. Jesus loves me. He set me free. My roots grow strong and deep down into Him.

God forbid that I should boast
except in the cross
of our Lord Jesus Christ.

Galatians 6:14

The Message

November 26

I can tell my friend about God's blessings. I can tell him all about the good things God can do. That is good. And I should tell him. But it is what Jesus did on the cross that will change his heart.

May I never boast about anything except the cross of our Lord Jesus Christ.

Galatians 6:14 NLT

In It But Not of It

November 27

Jesus lived in the world. He did not live far away in a place by Himself. The things of this world did not drive Him away from God. Jesus did not come to this world to get things. Jesus came here to get me. He wanted us to be friends.

Because of that cross, my interest in this world has been crucified, and the world's interest in me has also died.

Galatians 6:14 NLT

For Rich or for Poor

November 28

I can never earn God's love. I won't ever deserve it—no matter what I say or do. God's love is a gift. He gives it for free! It can never be bought. All I have to do is take it.

Because of Christ Jesus,
he freely accepts us and sets us
free from our sins.

Romans 3:24 CEV

That Explains It!

November 29

I want to be a Christian—a real Christian. Not just a nice person who goes to church a lot. A person whose life cannot ever be explained—except by Jesus. I want to be such good friends with Jesus that people will see Him when they look at me.

"He will glorify Me."

John 16:14

I Am What I Am

November 30

I am not a saint. Or am I? Sometimes what
I really mean is "God can never make a saint out
of me!" And God most certainly can. So that is
not the question. The question is, will I let Him?

His grace toward me
was not in vain.

1 Corinthians 15:10

That Is the Gospel

December 1

Have I broken God's commandments? God is not pleased. I must be punished. That is the law! But Jesus took my place. He said, "Punish Me instead." That is the gospel! The price has been paid to take my sins away. I am not a prisoner of sin anymore. I am free!

For whoever shall keep
the whole law. . .

James 2:10

Just Right!
December 2

Am I trying to be the perfect Christian?
Am I working hard to put on a pretty show?
If my heart is set on me, people will be drawn
to me. But if I give my heart to Jesus, people
will be drawn to Him.

Not that I have already attained,
or am already perfected. . .

Philippians 3:12

Getting to Know You

December 3

I want to share Jesus. I want my friends to know Him, too. But what is the best way to do it? With smart words? With fancy stories? The very best way to share Jesus with my friends is to get to know Him myself.

My speech and my preaching were not with persuasive words.

1 Corinthians 2:4

Be Glad

December 4

Jesus said trouble would come. But did He say, "Give up"? No. He said, "Be glad, for I have defeated everything that will ever try to hurt you." And He did! But to do it, Jesus had to fight all the bad things. So I will fight them, too. I will fight to do right. And I will be glad!

"To him who overcomes. . ."

Revelation 2:7

His Temple

December 5

My body is God's temple. Jesus lives here. Do I take care of His temple? Or do I let it see and hear and do things that would break God's heart?

"Only in regard to the throne will I be greater than you."

Genesis 41:40

Rainbow

December 6

God made a promise. But do I believe it?
I say, "Do something, God, and then I will trust
You." God says, "Trust Me, and then I will do
something!" It's up to me now. Jesus is waiting.
Will I give Him my heart?

"I set My rainbow in the cloud."

Genesis 9:13

I'm Sorry

December 7

I have sinned. I hurt myself. And I hurt my friend. But I hurt Jesus most of all. For it is against Him and Him only that I have sinned. Please forgive me, God. I am sorry. I want to change. I want to be like You.

Godly sorrow produces repentance leading to salvation.

2 Corinthians 7:10

So Deep

December 8

Jesus forgave me! I should not be forgiven.
I deserve to be punished. But God forgives
me anyway! Because of the cross. Because
of His Son. Jesus' death lets God forgive me.

By one sacrifice he has made
perfect forever those who are
being made holy.

Hebrews 10:14 NIV

It's Only Natural

December 9

It's only natural to want to do the right thing. And there are many good things I can do. But I must never let those good things keep me from doing God's best. Sometimes God wants me to do more than pray. He wants me to do something for Him!

Those who belong to Christ Jesus have nailed the passions and desires of their sinful nature to his cross.

Galatians 5:24 NLT

What I Want

December 10

There are many things I want. There are some I want right now. But what does God want? God wants the very best for me. When I give God my wants, He will give me what I need!

Abraham had
two sons.

Galatians 4:22

Delicious!

December 11

My special talents and gifts are like the husk on a delicious ear of corn. They are a wonderful part of me. But they are the outside. To get to the beautiful gold inside, I must let Jesus peel my husk away.

"If anyone desires
to come after Me,
let him deny himself."

Matthew 16:24

Tip of the Iceberg

December 12

I whisper, "I can't," and God whispers, "You can." I'm alone and afraid. But He whispers, "Fear not," as He leads me into the darkness. What can God see that I cannot? He can see into my heart. He can see Jesus.

". . .that they may be one just as We are one."

John 17:22

His Place—Her Place

December 13

I want to pray for her. But where do I begin?
Do I put myself in her place? No! Her place is
a mess! I must put myself in God's place. I can't
fix her broken heart. She can't fix it either. But
God can. So I will pray. And soon she will come
running home to Him.

Men always ought to pray
and not lose heart.

Luke 18:1

Planting Peace

December 14

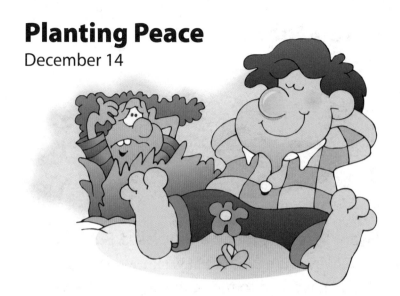

Did I do what Jesus asked? Then God's blessing will be peace. Did I do something else? Yes, I have pulled up all God's peace. I planted worry in its place. Now I have to pull up the worry and wait. Soon I will see what God will do next!

"Let not your heart be troubled."

John 14:27

Good Job

December 15

I want to tell my friend about Jesus. But I'm not always sure what to say. I know what others have said to me. And they have been very helpful. But now I must find a way to say it for myself—in my own words and in my own way. My friend may not listen to others. But I know she will listen to me. So I will not be afraid. I will tell her!

. . .a worker who does not need to be ashamed and who correctly handles the word of truth.

2 Timothy 2:15 NIV

Let's Wrestle!

December 16

God wants me to wrestle. But not with Him! I could get hurt! He wants me to wrestle in prayer—to pray and pray until the thing I'm praying for yells, "I give up—you win!"

Take up the whole armor of God. . . praying always.

Ephesians 6:13, 18

If I Be Lifted Up

December 17

What do I need? I need Jesus. But how do I know? Because someone told me! Now Jesus says, "Tell your friend. Tell him about Me. Tell him I died to set him free. Introduce Me to Him."

But the natural man
does not receive the things
of the Spirit of God.

1 Corinthians 2:14

This Day

December 18

This day is in God's hands. Tomorrow will be, too. I don't ever have to worry. Things will change. But that's okay. Jesus loves me. I can trust Him. He knows what to do.

All things work together
for good to those who love God.

Romans 8:28

Think about It

December 19

She says she is happy without Jesus. She does not want to change. That's not so strange. Anyone can be happy without Jesus. Jesus did not die to make me happy. Jesus died to make me His. He died to bring me home. He died to take away my selfishness and make me full of love. Sometimes that hurts. Sometimes it doesn't make me happy at all. But I want to be friends with Jesus more than I want anything else.

"I did not come to bring peace but a sword."

Matthew 10:34

One Way
December 20

There are many roads. And each one will lead me somewhere. But will it lead me to God? Whatever road I take, I want it to lead me to Jesus. I don't want to go anywhere else. I want people to see Jesus in my life.

"If I am lifted up from the earth, will draw all peoples to Myself."

John 12:32

I'm Sure!

December 21

Am I sure of myself? Or am I sure of God?
God has been so good. Together we have done
and seen amazing things. But I must never begin
to trust in the things I've done. Those things are
good. But they are not my God.

. . .that we might know
the things that have been
freely given to us by God.

1 Corinthians 2:12

Here I Come!

December 22

Did Jesus say, "Come"? Then I will come. I won't ask around to see what other people think. Do they know better than God? Of course not. How silly! And neither do I. So look out, Jesus— here I come!

> "No one can come to Me unless the Father who sent Me draws him."
>
> John 6:44

Good for You

December 23

O Lord, You're so good. Your tender love has completely changed my heart. You've made it alive and warm and new. My old heart is gone! Now I'm no good for hate. And I'm useless for sin. The only thing I'm good for is You.

God forbid that I should boast
except in the cross
of our Lord Jesus Christ.

Galatians 6:14

Hidden with Him

December 24

I am safe. Jesus is here. There is room to live. There is room to grow. Doubt Him? I dare you! Worry? Just try! I am safe. I am His. Jesus is here.

Your life is hidden with Christ in God.

Colossians 3:3

Happy Birthday!

December 25

Jesus Christ was born into our world on Christmas Day. But where does Jesus live today? Jesus wants to live inside of me—in my heart. When I let Him in, He is born in me, and I am born again!

"Behold, the virgin shall conceive and bear a Son."

Isaiah 7:14

Love Light

December 26

When Jesus died on the cross, He took away all of my sin. Sin moved out and Jesus moved in! Now I just want to be closer and closer to Him.

The blood of Jesus Christ
His Son cleanses us from all sin.

1 John 1:7

What to Do

December 27

God wants me to trust Him. I don't always know the right thing to do. But God knows. He will show me. All I have to do is ask. I can trust the Word of God. And when I do, my life will shine with the light of His love.

"If you will return, O Israel," says the LORD. . .

Jeremiah 4:1

Made Fresh Daily

December 28

God wants to change my heart. He wants me to be more like Jesus. Is there a part of me that is not like Jesus yet? I will let God change it. Every day I will let God make me a little bit more like Jesus.

"Unless you are converted and become as little children. . ."

Matthew 18:3

A True Believer

December 29

It's not always easy to do what God asks. The Bible tells me to love and pray for the people who hurt me. I don't always want to do that. But I will do what God tells me to do. He will help me. I will not turn my back on Him. I am a true believer!

Many of His disciples
went back.

John 6:66

Me, Me, Me, Me!

December 30

God made me special. There is no one else just like me. I can do many things very well, and God loves me just the way I am. But do you know what He loves most of all? He loves to see me becoming more and more like Jesus.

"All my springs are in you."

Psalm 87:7

Yesterday
December 31

I know God has good things planned for me in the New Year. But oh my—I made so many mistakes this year! How can Jesus love me when I don't do things right? I just don't know. But Jesus will forgive me. I can't change the things I did yesterday. I will leave yesterday with Jesus. I will walk right out into the New Year. I know Jesus will be with me. He is already waiting for me there!

The God of Israel
will be your rear guard.

Isaiah 52:12

INDEX

Ability of God: 2/29, 4/17, 7/20, 8/14, 11/6

Anger: 2/15, 6/30, 9/15, 9/26, 11/7

Being Born Again: 1/15, 1/20, 8/8, 8/15, 11/12, 12/25

Being Clean Inside: 3/18, 6/28, 8/17, 9/1, 9/15, 10/5

Being Like Jesus: 1/9, 1/17, 1/23, 2/8, 5/4, 6/7, 6/12, 6/15, 7/7, 9/1, 9/2, 9/27, 10/15, 11/29, 12/20, 12/28, 12/30

Being Used by God: 2/19, 2/20, 2/21, 3/4, 4/18, 4/23, 5/1, 5/8, 5/14, 5/20, 6/15, 7/9, 8/4, 8/17, 8/18, 8/30, 9/7, 9/11, 9/24, 9/30, 10/13, 10/14, 10/25, 10/26, 11/10

Belonging to Jesus: 1/21, 3/17, 5/29, 7/2, 7/15, 7/30, 9/4, 9/20

Bible, the: 1/3, 1/11, 3/10, 4/1, 4/7, 6/5, 6/28, 7/25, 7/27, 9/27, 10/10, 12/27, 12/29

Blessings of God: 2/4, 4/4, 4/9, 11/11, 11/17, 12/14

Busyness: 2/13, 10/19

Caring: 2/2, 2/3, 3/3, 3/30, 7/12

Closeness of God: 5/27, 5/28, 6/25, 7/29, 8/31, 9/5, 10/2, 11/16, 11/25, 12/24

Confusion: 1/12, 1/19, 9/12, 9/14

Creations of God: 1/9, 2/10, 2/11, 5/16

Criticism: 6/17

Desires of God: 1/8, 1/17, 3/8, 3/28, 5/12, 6/2, 6/5, 6/8, 8/19, 9/30, 10/25, 11/5, 12/9, 12/10, 12/27, 12/28

Disobedience: 1/28, 1/29, 2/15, 3/23, 11/19, 12/1

Doing God's Will: 1/1, 1/8, 1/16, 1/29, 1/30, 2/12, 2/26, 3/5, 3/20, 3/26, 4/15, 5/10, 5/13, 5/30, 7/18, 8/25, 8/27, 9/11, 10/8, 10/18, 10/21, 11/2, 11/3, 11/4, 11/10, 11/17, 11/18, 12/5, 12/22, 12/29

Doing Good Things: 1/18, 1/31, 2/5, 2/9, 3/1, 3/13, 3/17, 4/24, 4/27, 5/1, 7/11, 7/17, 7/22, 7/24, 9/9, 10/9, 12/2, 12/9

Doing Things My Way: 1/28, 1/29, 2/28, 5/4, 5/7, 6/27, 11/5, 11/15

Dreams: 2/20, 7/6, 9/23

Eternal Life: 4/12, 5/17, 9/21

Everyday Life: 3/6, 3/22, 5/9, 6/16, 10/17

Faith: 3/28, 4/21, 5/30, 7/29, 8/16, 8/29, 10/30, 10/31, 11/24

Fear: 3/7, 3/15, 4/20, 5/19, 5/24, 5/27, 6/5, 6/14, 8/2, 12/12

Feelings: 1/12, 2/27, 4/16, 5/20

Following God: 1/4, 1/5, 2/5, 2/24, 3/9, 3/15, 3/19, 3/28, 4/29, 6/8, 6/13, 6/16, 7/7, 7/8, 9/14, 9/19, 10/12, 10/30, 11/14, 11/22

Forgiveness from God: 2/18, 2/23, 2/28, 3/21, 4/5, 4/8, 4/20, 5/24, 8/24, 9/8, 10/28, 11/19, 11/20, 12/7, 12/8, 12/31

Forgiveness of Others: 6/22, 6/30, 7/14, 9/25, 9/26

Friendship with God: 1/7, 1/24, 2/8, 3/2, 6/3, 8/4, 8/16, 8/19, 8/21, 8/25, 9/21, 10/9, 11/27, 11/29, 12/19

Frustration: 2/16

Future, the: 1/2, 9/23, 10/14, 12/18

Gifts from God: 1/6, 1/10, 1/22, 2/4, 10/31, 11/28, 12/11

Giving to God: 3/12, 3/13, 3/14, 4/25

Hearing God's Voice: 1/1, 1/13, 1/16, 1/17, 1/30, 2/12, 2/13, 4/7, 5/13, 8/13, 9/10, 9/22, 10/8, 11/4, 11/17, 11/22

Help from God: 2/6, 2/9, 2/16, 2/17, 2/27, 4/13, 5/19, 6/6, 7/5, 9/5, 9/6, 9/17, 10/3, 10/24, 11/6, 12/4, 12/11

Hurts: 2/1, 2/23, 4/14, 5/31, 7/14, 7/30, 9/25

Inviting Jesus into My Heart: 4/11, 6/10, 9/13

Jesus' Death on the Cross: 4/5, 4/6, 4/8, 10/7, 10/28, 10/29, 11/19, 11/21, 12/1, 12/8, 12/26

Knowing God: 3/27, 7/11, 9/10, 10/27, 12/3

Letting God Change Me: 1/12, 3/16, 3/31, 4/3, 4/13, 5/8, 5/12, 5/31, 6/1, 7/1, 7/7, 7/15, 7/21, 7/26, 7/31, 8/14, 8/22, 8/28, 9/8, 9/28, 10/4, 10/13, 10/20, 11/12, 11/30, 12/11, 12/23, 12/28

Loneliness: 1/13, 1/19, 5/22, 7/13, 8/11

Looking for God: 2/14, 3/29, 4/4, 4/7, 6/9, 10/13

Loving Others: 2/3, 2/25, 3/3, 4/24, 5/11, 6/19, 9/20, 10/23, 12/29

Mistakes: 2/18, 3/23, 4/3, 5/24, 6/4, 7/3, 7/31, 10/6, 12/31

Obeying God: 1/11, 7/19, 7/27, 9/9, 9/22, 10/9

Patience: 3/11, 5/2, 5/6, 10/13

Plans of God: 1/17, 3/5, 3/11, 7/28, 8/3, 9/29, 10/25, 11/1, 12/31

Prayer: 1/4, 1/25, 1/30, 2/7, 3/30, 3/31, 4/1, 5/3, 5/25, 5/26, 5/29, 6/20, 6/21, 8/9, 8/24, 8/28, 9/5, 9/16, 10/11, 10/16, 10/17, 11/7, 11/8, 11/23, 12/13, 12/16

Provision from God: 1/26, 1/27, 5/16, 5/21, 6/26, 7/23, 8/6

Seeing Jesus: 4/2, 4/5, 4/8, 6/18, 8/12

Selfishness: 2/23, 4/30, 6/11, 6/12, 6/22, 6/23, 6/24, 7/3

Sharing: 1/6, 5/15, 9/2, 9/3

Sin: 4/10, 6/23, 6/24, 6/29, 9/24, 10/7, 10/23, 10/29, 11/19, 11/21, 12/1, 12/7

Staying Close to God: 4/19, 5/19, 5/22, 8/7, 8/23, 9/10, 10/9, 12/26

Talking with God: 1/3, 1/13, 8/6, 8/20

Telling Others about God's Love: 1/14, 2/1, 2/2, 2/3, 2/15, 2/25, 3/10, 3/17, 3/24, 3/25, 4/24, 5/5, 5/6, 6/28, 7/10, 8/1, 10/1, 10/14, 10/15, 10/16, 10/27, 11/9, 11/26, 12/3, 12/15, 12/17

Temptation: 9/17, 9/18, 9/19

Trusting God: 2/11, 2/22, 2/26, 3/15, 3/28, 4/17, 4/22, 4/26, 5/9, 5/10, 5/20, 5/23, 5/30, 6/14, 8/5, 8/26, 8/29, 9/12, 9/22, 10/11, 11/11, 11/13, 11/14, 11/24, 12/6, 12/18, 12/21, 12/24, 12/27

Worrying: 1/27, 2/7, 4/20, 4/28, 5/18, 5/21, 5/23, 6/2, 6/14, 6/21, 7/4, 7/16, 8/20, 8/26, 9/14, 10/18, 10/22, 12/14

Write to Phil A. Smouse

Once upon a time, Phil A. Smouse wanted to be a scientist. But scientists don't get wonderful letters and pictures from friends like you. So Phil decided to draw and color instead! He and his wife live in southwestern Pennsylvania. They have two children they love with all their heart.

Phil loves to tell kids like you all about Jesus. He would love to hear from you today! So get out your markers and crayons and send a letter or a picture to:

Phil A. Smouse
Barbour Publishing, Inc.
1810 Barbour Drive
Uhrichsville, OH 44683

Or visit his website at http://www.philsmouse.com/
and send him an e-mail at: phil@philsmouse.com.